THE HISTORY OF ROCKETS

THE **HISTORY** OF **ROCKETS**

by Ron Miller

A Venture Book

Franklin Watts
A Division of Grolier Publishing
New York   London   Hong Kong   Sydney
Danbury, Connecticut

This book is gratefully dedicated to
Jack Coggins, author and artist;
Charles Houchin, elementary teacher;
and Don Herbert (Mr. Wizard)
who together inspired my childhood interest
in space travel, astronomy, and science.

Photographs ©: Archive Photos: 61 (New York Times Co.), 27 (Popperfoto), 40; Corbis-Bettmann: 18, 88 right, 92 left; Lockheed Martin: 111; NASA: 80, 81, 83 right, 88 left, 93 right, 103; National Air and Space Museum: 30, 52, 54, 98 (Smithsonian Institution), 44, 47; North Wind Picture Archives: 13; Photo Researchers: 106 (Photo Aerospatiale/SPL), 87, 100; Photri: 74, 88 center; UPI/Corbis-Bettmann: 42, 49, 65, 68, 71, 83 left, 84, 85, 92 right, 93 left, 93 center; USAF Photo: 3, 9, 17, 26, 43, 53, 62, 64, 77, 97, 109.

Illustrations created by Victory Productions/Susan Littlewood

Library of Congress Cataloging-in-Publication Data

Miller, Ron
    The history of rockets / Ron Miller.
    p. cm. — (Venture book)
    Includes bibliographical references and index.
    Summary: Surveys the invention, development, and different uses of rockets, from their beginnings in ancient Greece and China to modern efforts to explore space.
    ISBN 0-531-11430-9 (lib. bdg.)   0-531-15962-0 (pbk.)
    1. Rockets—History—Juvenile literature. 2. Rockets (Aeronautics)— Juvenile literature. [1. Rockets (Aeronautics) 2. Outer space— Exploration.] I. Title.
TL782.5.M45 1999
621.43'56—dc21   97-49808
                                                        CIP
                                                        AC

©1999 by Ron Miller
All rights reserved. Published simultaneously in Canada.
Printed in the United States of America.
1 2 3 4 5 6 7 8 9 10 R 08 07 06 05 04 03 02 01 00 99

GROLIER
PUBLISHING

CONTENTS

THE HISTORY OF ROCKETS

1

WHAT IS A ROCKET?

What is the first image that comes to mind when someone says the word "rocket"? You probably think of the spacecraft that have landed on the Moon or surveyed the planets. You may also think of the **space shuttles**. But what exactly is a rocket? A rocket is a type of engine. It can produce more power for its size than any other kind of engine. In fact, a rocket engine can produce 3,000 times more power than a car engine of the same size. The word "rocket" may also be used to describe a spacecraft powered by a rocket engine.

How a Rocket Works

In the late 1600s, an English scholar and scientist named Isaac Newton developed three laws to explain how and why objects on the ground and in Earth's atmosphere move. The third of these laws applies to rockets. The law states that for every action, there is an equal and opposite reaction. In other words, when something is pushed forward, something else must move backward the same amount.

Here's an example. When a gun fires, the force of exploding gunpowder propels a bullet out of the barrel. At the same time, the gun **recoils** in the opposite direction. The action of the bullet flying out of the gun is balanced by the equal and opposite reaction of the gun's recoil. At this point, you are probably asking another question. If the opposite forces are supposed to be equal, then why doesn't the gun move as fast as the bullet?

The answer to this question lies in Newton's Second Law of Motion. It says that a heavy object **accelerates** more slowly than a light object. Because a gun weighs a lot more than a bullet, the force of the gunpowder does not propel the gun as fast as it shoots the bullet.

Unlike most guns, an automatic weapon, such as a machine gun, is designed to deliver a steady stream of bullets until the shooter stops pressing the trigger. As the weapon fires, it recoils continuously. You can experience the same effect by holding a garden hose while wearing in-line skates. The steady stream of water from the hose is equivalent to the steady stream of bullets from an automatic weapon. The recoil from the water will move your skates—and you—in the opposite direction. The faster the water leaves the nozzle, the faster you will move.

The exhaust of a rocket works exactly like that steady stream of water. The gas molecules that make up exhaust are produced as **fuel** is burned inside the rocket's engine. The forces of action and reaction, which propel the rocket forward, occur the moment the fuel is burned—before the exhaust leaves the engine. The movement of a rocket does not depend on anything outside the engine. ***In other words, a rocket is not propelled forward because its exhaust pushes against air.*** This is an important idea because space is a **vacuum**—it contains no air. In space, there is absolutely nothing to push against.

See for Yourself

If you're still unsure how Newton's Third Law of Motion applies to rockets, try the following experiment. Blow up a balloon. As more and more air enters the balloon, the air pressure inside it increases. If you let go of a fully blown-up balloon, air rushes out in one direction. The balloon reacts by moving in the opposite direction. The balloon shoots through the air because it is obeying Newton's Third Law of Motion. The balloon is behaving like a rocket.

You can make your balloon-rocket move in a straight line by taping a soda straw to the balloon and running a string through the straw. If you tie the ends of the string to two objects, such as two door knobs, the balloon will zip along the string in a straight line. To make a device that looks even more like a real rocket, place a sausage-shaped balloon inside a cardboard tube (from a roll of paper towels) and attach cardboard fins.

A rocket works better in a vacuum because there is no air to get in the way of the exhaust. Anything that slows the exhaust slows the rocket. Ultimately, a rocket's maximum speed and **payload**—how much it can carry—are determined by its **thrust**—how hard the engine can push.

See for Yourself

To measure the thrust of a homemade rocket, you will need a kitchen scale, tape or modeling clay, a small plastic bottle (an empty dish-washing detergent or shampoo bottle works fine) and a cork that fits on top, vinegar, baking soda, a tablespoon, and a measuring cup. *Caution: This experiment can be dangerous. It should be done under adult supervision.*

Using tape or modeling clay, fasten the bottle to the platform of the scale. Add 1 tablespoon (15 mL) of baking soda to the bottle. Quickly add $\frac{1}{4}$ cup (60 mL) of vinegar and place the cork on top of the bottle. Now stand back and watch what happens to the scale.

When the baking soda and vinegar mix, they produce carbon dioxide gas. The pressure of the gas builds up inside the bottle until the cork can no longer hold it in. The cork pops out, releasing the gas.

What happens to the scale when the cork popped out of the bottle? Does the bottle suddenly appear to "weigh" more? The change in the scale's reading is equal to the thrust of your rocket.

Who Invented the Rocket?

Because we have been exploring space for only a few decades, you might think that rockets must be a fairly recent invention. They aren't. Rockets have been around for a very long time. And they have been—and are still—used for more than just launching spacecraft.

More than 2,300 years ago, a Greek scientist named Archytas of Tarentum built a wooden pigeon and hung it from the ceiling using a long cord. When compressed air (or steam, depending on which version of the story you read) escaped from a hole in the pigeon's tail, the bird "flew" in circles. About 400 years later, Hero of Alexandria designed a device called an "aeolipile." Steam was fed into a hollow copper sphere in the device through pipes connected to a boiler. When the steam escaped from the sphere, the aeolipile rotated at a high speed. Both of these gadgets—the wooden pigeon and the aeolipile—were powered by primitive rockets. Although the Greeks invented the first rockets, they did not appreciate their usefulness.

About 800 years ago, the Chinese made the first practical use of rockets. They realized that rockets could be used as weapons. Their rockets were powered by a fuel that was

This drawing shows the aeolipile designed and built by Hero of Alexandria.

13

very similar to the gunpowder we use today. Gunpowder was invented by the Chinese about 1,100 years ago. Historians believe that it was first used to make fireworks for celebrations and festivals. The powder was rolled in paper and each end of the paper was tightly twisted. When these firecrackers were lit, they exploded with a flash and a bang.

Sometimes gases escaped from the ends of poorly wrapped firecrackers, so that they shot through the air instead of exploding on the ground. Eventually, the Chinese decided to make firecrackers that would always shoot through the air, so they intentionally left one end of the paper open. The resulting firecracker rockets moved in the direction opposite the end that was left unwrapped.

Making firecracker rockets involved a great deal of skill and patience. They had to be designed so that the gunpowder burned at just the right speed. If it burned too quickly, the rocket would explode without shooting through the air. If it burned too slowly, the rocket would fizz and sputter out on the ground. The gunpowder also had to be packed evenly and all the grains of powder had to be equal in size. If the gunpowder burned unevenly, the rocket would shoot around in all directions. It took a long time to figure out how to control a rocket. The Chinese had learned many lessons by the time they used them in warfare, but rockets were still far from perfect.

Improving the Rocket

Eventually, the Chinese learned that they could balance a rocket with a stick exactly seven times longer than the rocket—just as a pole can help a high-wire artist to balance. When the stick was inserted into the back end of the rocket, the rocket became reasonably accurate. In fact, this design is still used to make simple fireworks, such as bottle rockets.

While this new design was a tremendous improvement, it was still far from ideal. As the rocket burned fuel, its weight was redistributed. In other words, its **center of gravity** changed. The stick balanced the rocket at the start of its flight, but by the time the rocket had used most of its fuel, it was way out of balance.

As the Chinese continued to refine the rocket, they found that adding a cone-shaped nose had two advantages. First, it streamlined the rocket, so that it could fly a little faster. Second, it provided some space for a payload. If the rocket was launched during a celebration, the payload would consist of confetti or a special mixture of chemicals that created a beautiful burst of color. If the rocket was used in battle, the payload would consist of a powerful bomb.

The Chinese also discovered that a rocket worked better if it received a little less gunpowder at the beginning of its flight. Achieving this meant using a special technique to pack the gunpowder. First, a wooden cone, called a thorn, was placed on the rocket-maker's workbench, point up. A cardboard tube was then wrapped around the thorn, and a metal cylinder was placed over the cardboard to hold everything in place. After gunpowder was added from above, a powerful press packed the powder. When the rocket was removed from the metal cylinder, it consisted of a cardboard tube containing perfectly packed gunpowder with a cone-shaped hole at the bottom. To complete the rocket, the rocket-maker added a nose cone and a guide stick.

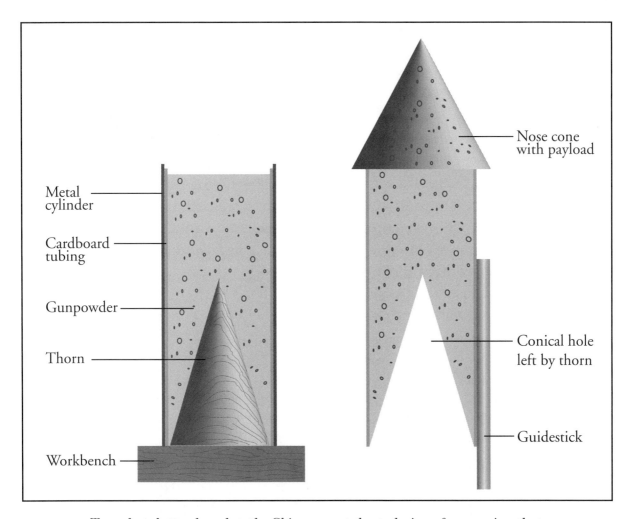

Metal
cylinder

Cardboard
tubing

Gunpowder

Thorn

Workbench

Nose cone
with payload

Conical hole
left by thorn

Guidestick

To make a better skyrocket, the Chinese created a technique for ensuring that less gunpowder was available at the beginning of the rocket's flight.

Even with all these improvements, rockets remained unpredictable and could only be used at close range. Despite these limitations, the Chinese—and later the Arabs—used rockets as weapons for many years. They also worked very well for fireworks displays and as signals.

2

THE ROCKET GOES INTERNATIONAL

Rockets in Europe

The first recorded use of the rocket in European warfare was at the siege of Chioggia, Italy, in 1379. The Italians called this unfamiliar weapon "rochetto" after the similarly shaped wooden bobbin or spool used in yarn-making. The British changed the Italian word "rochetto" into the English word "rocket."

Many Europeans experimented with rockets. Konrad Keyser, a German, launched a kite with a rocket. Joanes de Fontana, an Italian military engineer, filled a sketchbook with designs for new types of rocket-powered weapons. And Conrad Haas, a Romanian, came up with ideas of his own. He imagined two-staged rockets and rockets that could carry warheads designed to explode on impact. He was also the first to suggest using fins—rather than a long stick—to balance rockets.

European royalty was intrigued by fireworks and skyrockets. In 1680, Czar Peter the Great of Russia built a rocket factory in Moscow. Peter's army used the rockets as signals and to illuminate battlefields.

However, most monarchs were more interested in creating brilliant fireworks displays. Every occasion became an excuse to mount spectacular demonstrations. Famous composers were commissioned to write music to accompany the shows. Planning and financing fireworks displays quickly became a favorite pastime of kings, princes, and popes. Their fireworks exhibitions were larger and more elaborate than most of those seen today.

In 1699, the rulers of Austria sponsored an elaborate fireworks display to mark the eight-hundredth anniversary of the Abbey of Ranshofen.

The Italians were the first to develop **pyrotechnics**—the art and science of creating fireworks. Some families, such as the Ruggieris, became famous for their fireworks and carried this tradition through several generations.

The Indians Use Rockets

In the late 1700s, British armies were very busy. At the same time that they were fighting against the colonies in America, they were conquering the native peoples of India. Because the British were so powerful, the Indians were overwhelmed. In 1780, the British invaded Mysore, a city ruled by Rajah Hyder Ali. An inventor working for the rajah had solved many of the problems associated with rockets.

By making the tubes that held gunpowder out of iron instead of cardboard, the inventor had been able to construct very large rockets. These 12-pound (5.4-kg) rockets were stabilized with bamboo poles 10 feet (3 m) long and could travel more than 2,600 feet (792 m). When the British arrived, the rajah was ready. He launched hundreds of these rockets at a time. The astonished British troops retreated quickly.

William Congreve Begins to Experiment

News of the British defeat traveled quickly. A young British artillery colonel named William Congreve visited all the fireworks manufacturers in London and ordered their largest skyrockets. He wanted to see if he could make rockets that were even better than those used by the rajah. He soon developed large, powerful iron-cased rockets of his own.

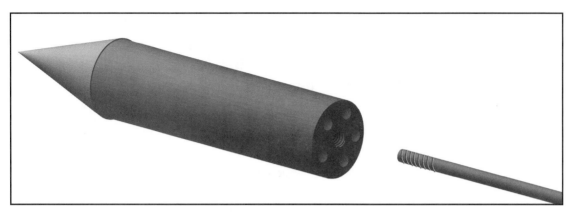

William Congreve's rocket had a wooden pole screwed into a hole between exhaust ports.

By 1805, Congreve had designed rockets that could carry a 6-pound (2.7-kg) lead ball more than 6,000 feet (1,829 m). He also invented explosive-filled nose cones that burst when they struck an object. Eventually, his rockets were 8 inches (20 cm) in diameter and weighed 300 pounds (136 kg)! They could travel more than 5,300 feet (1,615 m) and easily penetrate the walls of buildings.

Congreve also thought about accuracy. He moved the balance pole to the center of the base and allowed the exhaust to escape from five holes spaced around the pole. This improved the rocket's balance tremendously. The design also allowed soldiers to carry the stick separately and screw it into the base of the rocket just before launching the weapon. This made transporting rockets much easier.

The British army formed a special Mounted Rocket Corps that used rockets against very large targets, such as forts or cities. The nose cones of these rockets were filled with incendiary materials that started fires where they burst. The rockets were used for this purpose because, even with Congreve's improvements, they still weren't very reliable. But if enough rockets were launched in the right direction, it didn't matter if a few dozen went the wrong way. Most would land more or less on target.

The British navy liked Congreve's rockets because they were mobile, inexpensive, and lighter than cannons. Most importantly, they did not recoil. When a cannon blasts a heavy cannonball out of its muzzle, the cannon tries to fly off in the opposite direction. The greater the charge of gunpowder and the heavier the cannonball, the more forceful is the cannon's recoil. The heavy ropes and chains needed to keep cannons in place put a great deal of strain on the ships. Rockets did not have this problem.

On October 8, 1806, the British launched 200 Congreve rockets at Boulogne, a French seaport. The rockets set part of the city on fire. A year later, the British fleet attacked Copenhagen, Denmark, which was being held by Napoleon's forces. More than 25,000 rockets were launched, and the city was entirely destroyed.

When firing at land targets—such as a fortress or a city—the British navy launched rockets at a high angle, so that they would clear protective walls and drop on the roofs of buildings. But rockets used against other ships were launched nearly parallel with the surface of the water. They skipped like stones over the waves and, if all went well, blasted into one of the portholes of the enemy ships.

Using Rockets Against the United States

Rockets were also used by the British against the Americans during the War of 1812, but with much less success. In 1814, the

British navy attacked Fort McHenry, which protected the city of Baltimore, Maryland. Teams of three or four men rowed small rocket-launching boats close to shore, positioned a ladder to create a launching rack, and lit the rockets' fuses with the flint-lock from a gun. The crew dressed in heavy leather coats and hats to protect themselves from the tremendous rush of flames generated by the rocket exhaust.

Although hundreds of rockets were launched, the fort refused to surrender. The Americans considered this a great victory. Francis Scott Key, a poet who witnessed the bombardment, was inspired by the event. He was so impressed that the American flag continued to fly during "the rockets red glare" that he wrote a moving poem. Today every person in the United States knows the words of this poem because they were set to music and became the national anthem—"The Star-Spangled Banner."

Rocket Research Continues

Despite this defeat, Congreve continued to have high hopes for his rockets. Since they could fly much farther than cannonballs, he thought rockets would eventually replace them. Over the next few years, however, guns and cannons were improved more rapidly than rockets. Soon, cannons could fire farther than rockets and with much greater accuracy. Eventually, rockets were hardly used at all.

In 1839, a self-taught British engineer named William Hale began to think about improving the accuracy of rockets. He had a radical idea. He wanted to eliminate the balance stick alto-gether. Instead of a bamboo or wooden pole, Hale placed three small metal **vanes**—thin flat blades similar to those of a fan or

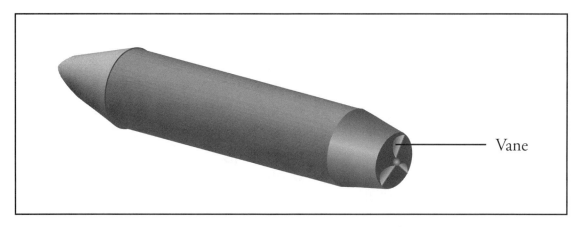

Vane

William Hale's rocket spun as exhaust shoot past the vanes.

propeller—in the path of the exhaust. Since each vane was attached to the rocket at a slight angle, they made the rocket spin as it flew. Hale patented his **rotary rocket** in 1844.

Hale's idea was based on the discovery that bullets are more likely to hit their target if they spin while in flight. To give bullets spin, manufacturers **rifle**—cut spiraling grooves inside—the barrels of guns and cannons. These grooves cause bullets to turn as they travel down the length of the barrel. And when the bullets leave the gun's muzzle, they are spinning rapidly. This spin makes the flight of the bullet very stable and accurate. Hale believed that a spinning rocket would fly farther, and straighter. He was right. In one trial, a Hale rocket traveled more than 2.5 miles (4 km) and landed only 30 feet (9 m) from its target.

Unfortunately, Hale's invention came too late. The military was thrilled with recent improvements in guns and cannons, and no longer had any interest in rockets. The successful experiments of Congreve, Hale, and inventors in France, Russia, Germany, Italy, and Austria, did, however, inspire new uses for rockets—uses that had nothing to do with either warfare or fireworks.

New Uses for Rockets

A life-saving rocket was used by the British to rescue people from sinking ships. One end of a rope was fastened to a stronghold on the rescue vessel, while the other end was attached to a the rocket. When the rescuers shot the rocket to the sinking ship, the rope was propelled across the water and the passengers on the sinking ship could use the rope to climb to safety. Between 1871 and 1962, more than 15,000 people were saved using these life-saving rockets.

Although Congreve designed the earliest life-saving rockets, they were refined by other inventors, such as John Dennett. Dennett's rockets were fired from lightweight, portable stands that could be set up and aimed by anyone. Some of his rockets were designed to snag themselves in a ship's rigging or to attach themselves to parts of the wreck—in case the ship's crew was too exhausted to attach the line themselves. Life-saving rockets are still used today.

In the 1800s, whaling was an important industry because oil from whale blubber was used to fuel lanterns. Whalers used rockets to shoot harpoons from the decks of their ships into the bodies of whales. Successful rocket attacks on whales were recorded as early as 1821, when the captain of the *Fame* boasted that he had caught nine whales with rocket harpoons.

In the mid-1800s, a whaling rocket was patented by Thomas Welcome Roys, a whaling captain, and Gustavus Adolphus Lilliendahl, a fireworks manufacturer. Thinking that the Roys-Lilliendahl rocket harpoon was not powerful enough, John Nelson Fletcher and Robert L. Suits designed their own rocket and began to sell it. The Fletcher-Suits rocket harpoon was 6.5

feet (2 m) long and weighed 32 pounds (14.5 kg). According to the manufacturers, it could hit a whale 180 feet (54.9 m) away. This made it considerably better than a hand-thrown harpoon.

Although rockets were no longer being used as military weapons, the French used them to illuminate battlefields at night. Rockets designed for this purpose could reach an altitude of 1,000 feet (305 m) and then release a parachute carrying a brilliant flare that lit up the ground below. During World War I, soldiers used similar rockets to send messages from one unit to another or from the front lines to a rear command post.

These rockets were used more than 50 years after Hale's improved rocket design, but they were still quite primitive. It looked as though all Hale's innovations were just being ignored. In fact, the rockets used during World War I were little different than those used by the Indian rajah against the British in 1780. It was not until the early days of World War II that the military began to take another look at rockets.

3

THE DREAMERS

The idea of launching rockets into space did not come from the people who invented or refined them, but from writers. In 1657, Cyrano de Bergerac published the first known fictional account of a man traveling into space in a rocket. In *A Comic History of the Continents and Countries of the Lunar Empire*, the author describes several highly imaginative—and humorous—methods for reaching the Moon. One of these methods involves the use of rockets.

It was not until 1852 that the idea of space travel powered by rockets appeared again. In *Gulliver Joi*, American writer Elbert Perce describes a rocket consisting of a long, metal cylinder with pointed ends. The rocket, which has a cockpit just large enough for one person, burns special fuel in a combustion chamber and emits exhaust through a nozzle at the rear. The hero of the story uses the rocket to travel to the planet Kailoo. Although this planet is entirely imaginary, the description of the rocket and its flight is extremely accurate. Unfortunately, very few people read Perce's book.

From the Earth to the Moon, published in 1865, received a lot more attention. In this book, French science-fiction writer Jules

Verne describes the process of building a spaceship. Although he suggested using a giant cannon to launch his spaceship—a very bad idea—he recommended using rockets to steer and control the vehicle while it was in space. Many people believed that Verne's story was true and wrote letters asking if they could travel in his spaceship!

Jules Verne's classic science fiction thriller From the Earth to the Moon *inspired generations of rocket scientists.*

27

Escape Velocity

Have you ever heard the saying, "What goes up must come down"? If this were always true, we'd spend a lot of time dodging falling satellites. The saying is true only for objects moving slower than **escape velocity**—the speed at which an object must travel to escape from Earth's gravity forever, or 7 miles/second (11.2 km/sec).*

If a projectile left the muzzle of a cannon at a speed of 7 miles/second (11.2 km/sec), it would never fall back to Earth. It would shoot off into space forever. It is just barely possible for a cannon to do this because the projectile has to attain its maximum speed while it's still inside the barrel. Once it leaves the cannon, it starts slowing down (due to air resistance).

Although scientists knew that Verne's book was fiction, it was so realistic that they were inspired. Many began to think that traveling into space might be possible, and they knew that rockets would be the best way to propel, steer, and brake a vehicle outside Earth's atmosphere. Verne had hit upon exactly the right idea.

From Fiction to Fact

Around the same time, Nikolai Ivanovich Kibalchich, a Russian political activist who had been involved in the assassination of

If scientists were only interested in propelling objects into space, a cannon with a very long barrel could be used. But this type of design could never be used to launch people into space. The human body could not withstand such rapid acceleration over such a short distance. Jules Verne's famous space gun, for example, was 900 feet (274 m) long. If human passengers accelerated from 0 to 7 miles/second (11.2 km/sec) over such a short distance, their bodies would have been spread into a thin film.

Rockets have a big advantage over a giant space gun. Because they can contain their own fuel and can have multiple stages, rockets can take off slowly and build up speed gradually until they reach escape velocity.

* Escape velocity varies depending on the body a rocket is lifting off from. Planets with more—or less—gravity than Earth have different escape velocities.

Czar Alexander II, was also thinking about using rocket-propelled vehicles. While in prison awaiting execution, Kibalchich worked out an idea for a strange type of flying machine—a platform with a railing all the way around it and a large hole in the center. A sort of giant machine gun would be mounted above the hole with its muzzle pointing down. By rapidly and continuously feeding dynamite cartridges into the gun, the platform would be lifted into the air. If the gun were placed in a swivel mount, the platform could be steered by moving the muzzle from side to side. All of Kibalchich's notes were filed away and rediscovered in 1918.

This drawing illustrates Hermann Ganswindt's concept for a space vehicle.

In 1893, Hermann Ganswindt, an eccentric German inventor, published his own rocket design. It consisted of a large, cylindrical passenger cabin suspended beneath a bullet-shaped engine. Ganswindt intended to fuel the rocket with thousands of heavy steel cartridges, each charged with a load of dynamite. When a cartridge was fired, half of it shot forward, passing through a round hole that ran through the passenger cabin. The other half of the cartridge was thrown against the inside of the firing chamber. Ganswindt mistakenly believed that the force of this last action would lift the spaceship. Although his details were wrong, his basic ideas were sound. Unfortunately, most people thought his ideas were ridiculous.

Konstantin Tsiolkovsky of Russia developed an interest in the idea of interplanetary flight while he was a teenager. Tsiolkovsky's father sent him to school in Moscow, and in 1878, he became a teacher. In his spare time, Tsiolkovsky performed experiments in a laboratory he had set up in his home. *From the Earth to the Moon* made a tremendous impression on him. Several years later, he wrote the following passage in his journal:

> For a long time, I thought of the rocket as everybody else did—just as a means of diversion and of petty everyday uses. I do not remember exactly what prompted me to make calculations of its motions. Probably the first seeds of the idea were sown by that great fantastic author Jules Verne—he directed my thought along certain channels, then came a desire, and after that, the work of the mind.

Tsiolkovsky sent his findings to the Society of Physics and Chemists in St. Petersburg, Russia. The members of this prestigious organization were so impressed with Tsiolkovsky's results that they asked him to join the society.

In 1883, Tsiolkovsky made a great discovery, which he wrote about in his journal on March 28 of that year.

> Consider a cask filled with a highly compressed gas. If we open one of its taps the gas will escape through it in a continuous flow, the elasticity of the gas pushing its particles into space will also continuously push the cask itself. The result will be a continuous change in the motion of the cask. Given a sufficient number of taps (say, six), we would be able to regulate the outflow of the gas as we liked and the cask (or sphere) would describe any curved line in accordance with any law of velocities . . . As a general rule, uniform motion along a curved line or rectilinear non-uniform motion in free space involves continuous loss of matter.

What Tsiolkovsky was describing was, of course, Newton's Third Law of Motion—as it applies to space travel. In 1898, he published his ideas in an article called "Exploration of Space with Reactive Devices." The article included mathematical calculations proving that it is possible to launch a rocket into space and steer it once it is beyond the atmosphere. Tsiolkovsky also discussed the benefits of **liquid-fuel rockets** and **multistage rockets**. He understood that liquid fuel would make it possible to build extremely powerful rockets with engines that could be stopped and then restarted. He also realized that multistage rockets could conquer gravity.

The pull of Earth's gravity is so great that 402 pounds (182 kg) of fuel are required for every 1 pound (0.5 kg) sent into space. This was a major obstacle because 402 pounds (182 kg) of fuel required a rocket weighing more than 1 ton. In other words, a rocketship's fuel tank alone would weigh too much for it to lift!

Tsiolkovsky was not the first scientist to realize the importance of multistage rockets. A number of early rocket theorists had suggested designs for rockets that become smaller as they move farther from Earth. This could be achieved if fuel tanks were released as the fuel and **oxidizer** inside were used up. Since the whole rocket would weigh less, the remaining tanks could be smaller.

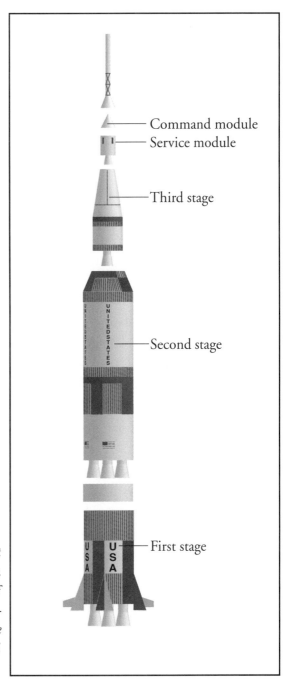

The Saturn 5 multistage rocket launched three astronauts to the Moon in 1969. The first and second stages of the rocket launched the Apollo spacecraft into space. The third stage put the spacecraft into orbit around Earth and then on course to the Moon.

Command module
Service module
Third stage
Second stage
First stage

According to this theory, if a rocket has three stages, the first one—called the **booster**—launches the rocket. The booster must be quite large because it has to lift not only itself but all the stages above it. When the booster uses up all its fuel, the vehicle drops that section and uses the second stage. The second stage can be somewhat smaller because it only has to lift itself and the third stage. The third stage could be even smaller because it only has to lift itself.

A multistage rocket also has another advantage—its speed is cumulative. Here's an example. If the top speed of each stage of a three-staged rocket is 100 mph (161 km/hr), the whole rocket will be traveling 100 mph (161 km/hr) at the point where the first stage drops away and the second stage starts. If the second stage were launched from a standing start, it could reach a maximum speed of only 100 mph (161 km/hr). However, since it is already going 100 mph (161 km/hr), its top speed will be 200 mph (322 km/hr). When the third stage starts, it will add its 100 mph (161 km/hr) to the rocket's 200 mph (322 km/hr) speed, so its final velocity will be 300 mph (483 km/hr).

Tsiolkovsky wrote detailed descriptions of all sorts of spacecraft—from space stations to lunar rovers. But because his early work was not translated into other languages, very few people knew about his ideas.

Hermann Oberth, a German physicist, had a very different experience. Like Tsiolkovsky, he was inspired by *From the Earth to the Moon*. At the age of 15, Oberth designed his first spaceship—a manned, multistage, **solid-fuel rocket**. He quickly realized that solid fuels were too weak for spaceflight and began looking for alternatives. He soon discovered the possibilities of liquid fuels, and by 1912, he had designed a rocket powered by liquid oxygen and liquid hydrogen.

Although Oberth studied at a number of universities, he never received a Ph.D. because his dissertation, which discussed spaceflight, was rejected. Like Tsiolkovsky, he became a schoolteacher and did research in his spare time. In 1923, he published his findings in a book called *The Rocket in Planetary Space.* The work contained mathematical calculations and technical drawings proving that a liquid-fuel, multistage rocket could work. Oberth described how such a spaceship could be built, steered, and navigated as well as how it would re-enter Earth's atmosphere and be recovered.

He also discussed the hazards of spaceflight and how humans could survive in space. He even described space stations and space telescopes. There was so much detail in the book that many readers felt that, by following Oberth's instructions, they could go out and build a spaceship.

Because Oberth's writing style was very complex and technical, many people had trouble understanding it. As a result, several popular science writers explained his ideas in simpler language, and Oberth became an overnight sensation. His ideas quickly spread through Germany and the rest of the world.

When Oberth wrote his book, he had four main goals. He wanted to prove

- that building a rocket capable of reaching the upper atmosphere was possible using available technology and materials;
- that, with "additional refinement," the same rocket could travel into outer space;
- that, with further modifications, rockets would be capable of carrying passengers;
- that these rockets could be made profitable.

A great many scientists disagreed with Oberth's ideas, but their debates made the general public even more interested in

Solid Fuel Versus Liquid Fuel

Most rocket motors operate by burning fuel within a combustion chamber. When hot gases escape through a narrow nozzle, the rocket is propelled forward. Solid fuel rockets burn a powdered substance that contains fuel and oxygen. Gunpowder is an example of a solid fuel. This type of rocket works equally well in Earth's atmosphere and in space.

Solid-fuel rockets are simple, powerful, and easy to store for long periods of time. On the other hand, they cannot be controlled. Once a solid-fuel rocket starts to burn, it's impossible to stop it. It's also impossible to control the burning. You can't slow the rocket down or speed it up.

The fuel and oxidizer for a liquid-fuel rocket are kept in separate containers. Powerful pumps force both liquids into the combustion chamber as they are needed. This type of rocket is more complicated and more difficult to build than a solid-fuel rocket. It requires special tanks to hold its **propellants**, a pump running from each tank to the engine, and motors to run the pumps. Storing liquid fuels for a long period of time is difficult, so these rockets must be fueled shortly before their launch.

Liquid fuels are much more powerful than solid fuels. In addition, it is possible to control a liquid-fuel motor. If you want to stop the motor, all you have to do is to stop the pumps. If you want to restart the motor, all you need do is ignite the propellants and start the pumps again. To control the rocket's speed, all you have to do is adjust the rate at which the fuel and oxidizer flow into the engine.

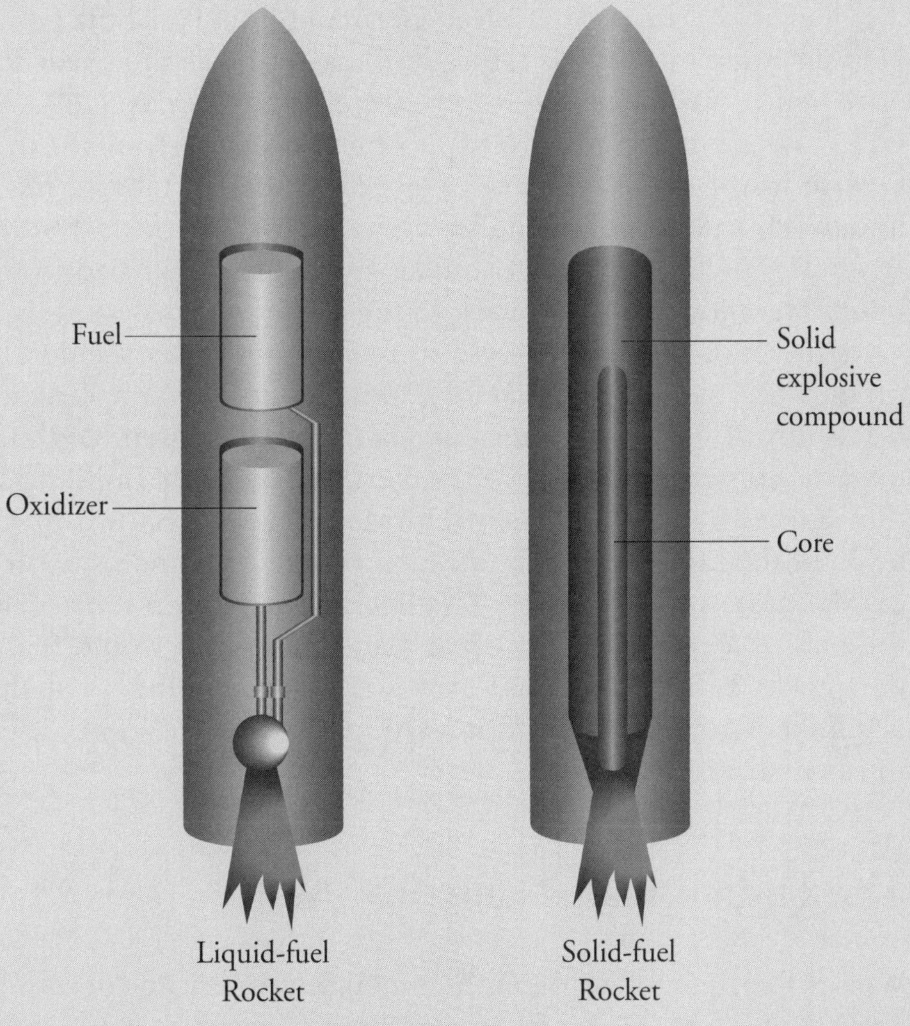

Fuel

Oxidizer

Solid explosive compound

Core

Liquid-fuel Rocket

Solid-fuel Rocket

the book. In fact, spaceflight became a fad and an international spaceflight movement began. Scores of magazine articles and books appeared, and rocket societies sprang up all over Europe. In 1929, Oberth published *The Way to Spaceflight*, which described his original ideas in much more detail and proposed additional theories.

Oberth's books even inspired German filmmaker Fritz Lang. He was as famous for his fantastic films—such as the great science-fiction epic, *Metropolis*—as George Lucas is today. He wanted to make a movie about a trip to the Moon and thought that Oberth would make the perfect technical adviser. Oberth readily agreed, and the spaceship he designed for the movie *Woman in the Moon* (1929) was very similar to the one described in his book. The movie is a landmark in the history of space travel.

Some parts of the film were so realistic that they seemed to predict the Saturn 5 *Apollo 11* Moon launch, which did not occur until 1969. In the movie, a giant rocket is assembled in a huge building very similar to the Vertical Assembly Building at the Kennedy Space Center in Florida where the Saturn 5 was built. In the film, the spacecraft is carried to its launch site on a crawler, just as Saturn 5 was. The fictional spaceship took off at the end of a countdown because Lang thought it would make the movie more dramatic. Forty years later, engineers at the National Aeronautics and Space Administration (NASA) used the same technique!

The United States Gets Involved

While Oberth was basking in the limelight, American rocket scientist Robert H. Goddard was making headlines of his own. Goddard began to think about rockets during his senior year of college. Unlike Tsiolkovksy, Goddard wanted to do more than think about rockets. He wanted to carry out actual experiments.

Goddard began by studying fireworks rockets because they were inexpensive and easy to obtain. Unlike his predecessors—Congreve and Hale—Goddard didn't shoot his rockets into the air. Instead, he tied them down and fastened them to measuring instruments. He wanted to determine their efficiency and the amount of power they produced.

In 1911, Goddard earned a Ph.D. from Clark University in Massachusetts, and began a 1-year research fellowship at Princeton University in New Jersey. He was thrilled. Now he could spend all his time studying rockets. Because funding for rocket research was limited, however, Goddard had to spend much of his own meager salary on equipment for his experiments.

The first thing Goddard realized is that the conical nozzle of an ordinary rocket loses its shape as the gunpowder burns away. To eliminate this problem, Goddard fashioned a steel nozzle that kept its shape. He also began using a more powerful smokeless type of gunpowder instead of ordinary black gunpowder.

Once he had improved the rocket design, Goddard performed a series of tests proving that a rocket could work in a vacuum. In 1916, he wrote a paper describing his experiments. He carefully explained how they proved that a rocket could reach the Moon, hoping that someone—or some organization—would be so impressed with his findings that they would fund his research.

When Charles Walcott, secretary of the Smithsonian Institution, read the paper he contacted Goddard and asked him how much money he would need. Goddard thought he would need at least $10,000. But since he was afraid to ask for that much, he requested $5,000. Goddard was astonished when the Smithsonian agreed and sent him a check for $1,000 as the first installment.

It wasn't long before Goddard's work was interrupted by World War I. He stopped working on a rocket that could reach the Moon, and developed designs for military rockets, including what eventually became the **bazooka**. After the war, he wrote a new paper—*A Method of Reaching Extreme Altitudes*—that included calculations showing that a multistage solid-fuel rocket weighing just 10 tons could carry a small payload of magnesium

A soldier demonstrates a new type of bazooka developed by the U.S. Army in 1964.

powder to the moon. This would create a flash bright enough to be seen from Earth, at least through a telescope.

Although fewer than 2,000 copies of this paper were printed, it immediately caught the attention of the press. Within a few months, dozens of magazines and newspapers carried the news of Goddard's "Moon rocket." To say that it caused a sensation would be an understatement. The quiet, unassuming professor suddenly became a national celebrity!

Goddard was criticized by some and praised by others. Many people thought that anyone who planned to send a rocket to the Moon had to be just plain nuts. On the other hand, quite a few people took Goddard's ideas seriously. In fact, he was deluged with letters from volunteers for the first flight!

Despite all the attention, Goddard focused on his research. Soon, he abandoned the idea of using solid-fuel rockets. He realized that no solid fuel could produce as much thrust as gasoline. Using a liquid fuel, however, introduced new problems. A liquid fuel like gasoline or alcohol demanded a separate source of oxygen. In other words, the rocket would need two containers—one for the fuel and one for the oxidizer. Goddard realized that he would also have to design a system to pump the liquids into the combustion chamber. By working diligently, Goddard was able to find solutions to these problems. In 1922, he successfully tested his new motor—the first liquid-fuel rocket motor in the world.

Over the next 4 years, Goddard built a complete rocket. What he constructed would hardly be recognized as a rocket today, though. It was a mass of tanks and pipes that looked more like modern sculpture than anything else. The whole thing was hardly 10 feet (3 m) tall. The motor, which was about 24 inches (61 cm) long, was situated at the top of the rocket. Below this were two cylindrical tanks—one containing gasoline, the other containing liquid oxygen. A cone-shaped asbestos cap kept the flame from the motor away from the fuel tank. Goddard used the pressure from the oxygen tank to force the liquids into the motor. It was an extremely dangerous design, but Goddard had built in a few safeguards.

On March 16, 1926, Goddard, his wife, and two assistants took the rocket to a nearby field. He filled and pressurized the tanks. Then he opened the valves and bravely held the flame of a blowtorch to the nozzle of the motor. The gasoline and oxygen ignited with a tremendous roar, and the rocket leaped from its launching stand. The rocket ran out of fuel 2.5 seconds later and fell back to Earth. It had traveled 184 feet (56 m) and reached a top speed of about 60 mph (100 km/hr). Although Goddard was hesitant to release the details of his work, news of what he had accomplished soon reached Europe.

Robert H. Goddard tested his first liquid fuel rocket in Auburn, Massachusetts, on March 16, 1926.

4

THE ROCKET SOCIETIES

The First Rocket Society

Even though European scientists weren't able to find out exactly how Goddard's rocket worked, news of the flight inspired them to work harder than ever. In 1927, a group of scientists in Breslau, Germany, decided to share their findings with one another. To formalize their agreement, they formed the Society for Spaceship Travel. The members of this society called themselves the VfR (an abbreviation of German words meaning "Society for Spaceship Travel"). The organization, which attracted members from all over Europe, had two primary goals—to educate the public about rockets and spaceflight and to build rockets.

The VfR accomplished the first goal by publishing a magazine called *The Rocket*. In addition, one of the society's most active members, Max Valier, wrote a book popularizing Hermann Oberth's ideas. Valier also wrote dozens of magazine articles and was an accomplished and popular lecturer. He had his own ideas about how to excite the public about the possibilities of rockets, many of which Oberth very much disagreed with.

How the society achieved its second ambition is a story all by itself. It began when Valier convinced a wealthy automobile manufacturer named Fritz von Opel to finance the building of a rocket-powered car. It was to be powered by solid-fuel rockets made by Friedrich Sander, who owned a factory that made rockets for signaling, life-saving, and other purposes. After a few false starts, Valier finally succeeded in driving a rocket-powered car at a speed of 55 mph (88.5 km/hr) for about 2,500 feet (762 m). The Opel Rak rocket car was a bullet-shaped vehicle with twelve large solid-fuel rockets mounted in the rear. A whole series of Opel Raks followed, numbered I through IV. The later rocket cars operated along railroad tracks.

Fritz von Opel behind the steering wheel of the rocket automobile "Rak 2" on May 23, 1928.

Old newsreels of the Opel Raks are spectacular, with the low-slung black cars trailing dense clouds of black smoke as they zoom around racetracks. Probably the most important experiment that Opel and Valier did—though almost no one realized it at the time—was to use Sander's rockets to propel an airplane. The first-ever manned rocket-powered airplane flight took place on June 11, 1928.

Although Valier's stunts certainly made news, they were not popular with everyone. Some members of VfR considered cars useless and claimed they did nothing to advance the cause of real rockets. While this may be true, Valier did succeed in bringing rockets to the attention of the public. Up until that time, most people associated rockets with nothing more than fireworks displays.

While Valier and Opel were performing their headline-catching stunts, Johannes Winkler, one of the leading members of the VfR, was building the first liquid-fuel rocket to be flown in Europe. It was successfully launched on March 14, 1931, and traveled to a height of 1,000 feet (305 m). Like Goddard's rocket, Winkler's looked more like a kite than a modern rocket. It consisted of an open framework of fuel tanks, pipes, and tubes with a small rocket motor at the top. It was only about 24 inches (61 cm) high and weighed 11 pounds (5 kg).

The most active members of the VfR were Rudolf Nebel, Klaus Riedel, Willy Ley, and a teenage genius named Wernher von Braun. Nebel and Riedel had already tried unsuccessfully to launch a rocket called the Mirak. Encouraged by Winkler's triumph, they forged ahead with Mirak III. The combined knowledge and experience of all four men went into the design of the new rocket. The first test of their entirely new rocket motor went extremely well. A few days later, the completed rocket was ready for its first flight.

Mirak III worked. It rose about 60 feet (18 m) before falling back to Earth. Four days later, the repaired rocket was ready for its second flight. According to Willy Ley,

> [Mirak III] took off with a wild roar. [It then] hit the roof of the building and raced up slantwise at an angle of about 70 degrees. After 2 seconds or so, it began to loop the loop, rose some more, spilled all the water out of the cooling jacket, and came down in a power dive.
>
> While it was diving, the wall of the combustion chamber—being no longer cooled—gave way in one place, and with two jets twirling it, the thing went completely crazy. [Amazingly enough, it] did not crash because the fuel happened to run out just as it pulled out of a power dive near the ground. Actually, it almost made a landing.

As it turned out, the rocket—which had soared to a height of 200 feet (61 m)—was almost undamaged after its wild flight. The rocketeers were ecstatic.

Willy Ley was so happy with the success of the experiment that he proposed abandoning the name "rocket," which he thought people associated with fireworks displays. He also wanted to come up with a new name that would distinguish the liquid-fuel rockets from the old solid-fuel ones. He proposed the name "repulsor," which had been used in a popular German science-fiction novel.

Repulsor II was even more successful than its predecessor. It rose to about the same altitude, but flew about 1,800 feet (549 m) horizontally, with none of the aerobatics that had made the flight of the Mirak III (Repulsor I) so exciting.

The Repulsor II ready for liftoff

A Rocket Society in the United States

The success of the VfR's work, and the fact that they published and distributed their results, inspired rocket experimenters all over the world—particularly in the United States. The American Rocket Society (ARS) was founded in 1930 by a group of science-fiction fans, writers, and editors. Initially, the members did not plan to conduct research. According to G. Edward Pendray, one of the society's founding members, "We believed generally that a few public meetings and some newspaper declarations were all that would be necessary to bring forth adequate public support for the spaceflight program."

The fledgling society got off to a slow start. In the 1930s, the group had very little money. The best it could do was report on the successful work of its European counterparts and promote the idea of space travel to the American public in its *Bulletin*. The ARS also scheduled a special U.S. premiere of the Fritz Lang movie, *Woman in the Moon*, at the American Museum of Natural History in New York City.

After a trip to Germany during which he visited with VfR members, Pendray was convinced that the ARS needed to start doing experiments. His first goal was to develop a workable rocket motor. The society's Experimental Committee estimated that this would cost $1,000—an enormous sum during those Depression years. Fortunately, liquid oxygen was donated by the Air Reduction Company and castings for the motor were donated by the Aluminum Company of America. So, with a little ingenuity, ARS members created a motor that cost only $49.50.

Other parts were obtained by more imaginative methods. By posing as "an interested manufacturer," one ARS member was able to obtain free valves. The aluminum water-jacket that surrounded and cooled the motor was a cocktail shaker given away as a premium by a chocolate-milk company. The parachute was sewn by Pendray's wife. And H. Franklin Pierce, who later became a president of ARS, did all the machine work in his own shop.

When it was completed, the rocket consisted of two parallel aluminum tanks that were 5.5 feet (1.7 m) long and 2 inches (5 cm) in diameter. One tank contained the fuel, the other contained the oxidizer. The 3-inch (7.6-cm)-diameter engine was made of aluminum. The rocket, including its four stabilizing fins, weighed 15 pounds (6.8 kg). Showing off the rocket at a lecture, Pendray grandly claimed that it ". . . is a start in the direction of interplanetary flight."

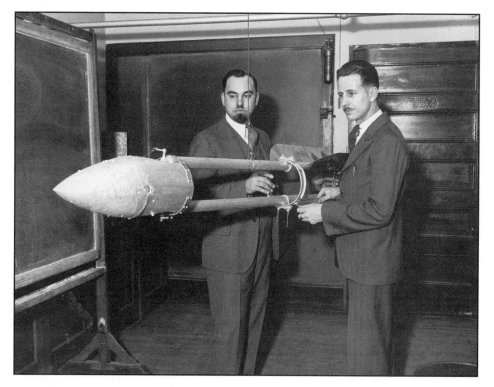

G. Edward Pendray (left) and H. Franklin Pierce (right) test the balance of their rocket on February 19, 1932.

In November 1932, the ARS built a wooden launch stand and two bomb-proof dugouts on a farm in Stockton, New Jersey. The dugouts were protected by piles of sandbags. Their first tests involved just the rocket motor. On November 12, Pendray lit the rocket's fuse (the electrical ignition system had failed). "With a furious hissing roar, a bluish white sword of flame shot from the nozzle of the combustion chamber, and the rocket lunged upward against the restraining springs." For 20 to 30 seconds the engine worked perfectly. Then the trouble began. Gasoline poured from the engine, creating a shower of fire all around the test frame.

The ARS members decided to try again. A redesigned rocket was launched on May 14, 1933, from the beach at Marine Park on Staten Island, New York. It rose to a height of about 250 feet (76 m) in 2 seconds. Then the oxygen tank burst and the rocket crashed. Nevertheless, the flight was considered a great success. It was the second liquid-fuel rocket launched in the United States.

Unfortunately, the ARS made only one other successful rocket flight before it ran out of money. After that, it concentrated on perfecting its motors. This was by no means a waste of time. In 1936, a motor designed by 23-year-old James Wyld made history. It solved one of the main problems associated with rocket motors—keeping them cool.

Most earlier rockets had been cooled by circulating water around them. While this design worked well enough for static tests, water jackets were much too heavy for flight. Wyld designed a motor that used fuel as the coolant. The motor was double-walled, with a space between the inner and outer walls. The fuel passed through this space before it was injected into the combustion chamber. This design was very clever because, while the fuel was cooling the engine, it was also being preheated so that it burned more efficiently. While this type of engine had already been developed in Europe, Wyld's motor was the first one in the United States. It was tested in 1938, and worked perfectly.

The ARS continued to flourish. By 1940, the organization had more than 400 members, including Robert Goddard. Eventually, it became the largest organization of professional rocket engineers in the United States. In 1963, it merged with the Institute of Aerospace Sciences to form a new organization called the American Institute of Aeronautics and **Astronautics** (AIAA). Today this group has more than 20,000 members.

A Rocket Society for the Soviet Union

While the VfR and ARS were designing and building rockets, the Society for the Study of Interplanetary Travel, was developing rockets in the Soviet Union. This organization, which is referred to as OIS (an abbreviation for Russian words meaning "Society for the Study of Interplanetary Travel"), was founded by an engineer named Friedrich Tsander and associated with one of the Soviet Union's most prestigious Air Force academies. Tsander's interest in spaceflight developed when he read the work of fellow-Russian Konstantin Tsiolkovsky. In fact, Tsiolkovsky was made an honorary member of OIS.

Unfortunately, OIS had a short life. Because the society had no funding, it could not finance research or publish a magazine like other groups. When an argument about Goddard's liquid-fuel rocket turned into a riot, the police had to be called in and the society was disbanded.

A few years later, a military research center involved in research of solid-fuel rockets moved from Moscow to Leningrad (now St. Petersburg) and was renamed the Gas Dynamics Laboratory. Soon after the move, a researcher named Valentin P. Glushko suggested that the laboratory begin to investigate and develop liquid-fuel rockets. The idea was approved, and Glushko headed the new division, which was called Department II.

Although the Gas Dynamics Lab was under the control of the Soviet army, one of Glushko's projects was the development of electric rockets. These rockets have almost no practical military use, but they are theoretically ideal for space travel.

Russian rocket scientists launched the GIRD-09 on May 17, 1933.

In the early 1930s, the Gas Dynamics Lab developed an impressive array of successful liquid-fuel rocket engines. Their OPM-52 was capable of generating 600 pounds (272 kg) of thrust, making it one of the most powerful rocket engines in the world. In 1933, the laboratory merged with the Group for the Study of Reactive Motion (GIRD) and became the Rocket Research Institute (RNII).

In 1934, a separate organization called the MosGIRD, because it formed in Moscow, joined the RNII and became aligned with the Soviet military. This group, formed in 1931 by Sergei P. Korolev, began as a small society of civilian experimenters but grew quickly. In August 1933, MosGIRD launched GIRD-09—the Soviet Union's first **hybrid rocket**. In November, it launched the GIRD-X—the Soviet Union's first true liquid-fuel rocket.

5

THE ROCKET AT WAR

At the end of World War I, the Allies forced the Germans to stop manufacturing a variety of weapons. As the Nazi party grew, its leaders encouraged scientists to develop new kinds of weapons that could be produced without violating their agreement with the Allies. As early as 1929, military researchers began to think about rocket-powered weapons. A young officer named Walter Dornberger was put in charge of rocket research and established a research facility near the town of Kummersdorf, Germany.

The VfR's experiments drew the attention of Dornberger and other members of the Nazi Party. The Nazis wanted the VfR to support them. One member, Rudolf Nebel, had already become a party member and urged his fellow rocketeers to join him. The VfR reluctantly aligned itself with the agenda of the Nazi Party.

Wernher von Braun, the VfR's young genius, became Dornberger's chief technical assistant. To his small group of experts, Dornberger added Walter Riedel, a highly experienced engineer, and a mechanic named Heinrich Grünow.

Dornberger was anxious to develop a motor far larger and more powerful than any of those tested by the VfR. After many months of hard work and several failures, the group built a motor that provided a steady thrust of 650 pounds (295 kg). Now the

Walter Dornberger was in charge of Peenemünde, the primary German rocket research center during World War II.

work really began. While part of the group worked on an even more powerful motor—one that could deliver 2,200 pounds (998 kg) of thrust—the others designed the missile that would be propelled by the motor.

First, the team had to solve the problem that had plagued rocket-makers for centuries—stability. Hale's method for achieving stability—spinning the entire rocket—would not work with a liquid-fuel rocket because **centrifugal force** would flatten the fuel against the walls of the tanks, and the engines would starve. Eventually, the scientists realized that it wasn't necessary to rotate the entire rocket. Even if only part of the rocket rotated, the entire missile would be stable. The 4.6-foot (1.4-m)-long rocket, which was named the Aggregate 1 (A-1) was designed so that its warhead spun rapidly on a shaft fitted with ball bearings.

The A-1 was never finished. Before the prototype was completely built, the researchers had designed a better rocket, the A-2. In December 1933, two A-2 rockets were tested on the island of Borkum in the North Sea. Each one soared to an altitude of about 6,500 feet (1,980 m).

Dornberger knew his team needed a new facility. He asked the government for more money and more space. (Military rocket research demands a great deal of wide-open space for safety—and for secrecy.) Von Braun suggested that the new research center be built on one of three small islands at the mouth of a river that emptied into the Baltic Sea. A few months later, the facility was built near the village of Peenemünde.

The first few rockets launched from Peenemünde had been designed at the old research facility. The A-3 model was more than 21 feet (6.4 m) long and 28 inches (71 cm) wide. The motor alone was 6 feet (1.8 m) long. Fully fueled, the A-3 weighed 1,650 pounds (748 kg). It was one of the largest, most ambitious rockets ever built. Unfortunately, it was a complete failure. The control system was nowhere near sensitive enough to guide the rocket.

After testing the A-3, the engineers had expected to design and construct their dream rocket—the giant A-4. But the A-3 failure meant that they faced months, perhaps years, of redesigning and testing. In the fall of 1939, shortly after World War II had started, the group successfully propelled a 1-ton rocket 5 miles (8 km) into the air. The rocket then floated back to Earth beneath a parachute. The scientists were finally ready to build the A- 4.

The A-4: A Rocketeer's Dream

The A-4 was larger, more complex, and more powerful than any previous rocket. It was as tall as a four-story building and weighed more than 14 tons. Its tanks contained nearly 10 tons of liquid oxygen and ethyl alcohol. The rocket's huge engine consumed all its fuel in just 68 seconds. By the time all the fuel was used, the rocket had achieved an altitude of 17.4 miles (28 km), traveling at a speed of 4,920 feet/second (1,500 m/sec). When the A-4 ran out of fuel, it continued to climb, reaching a maximum height of 50 miles (80 km).

On October 3, 1942, Dornberger's entire staff gathered to watch the first flight of the new A-4. The group knew that future funding depended on the rocket's performance. The takeoff was perfect. The giant rocket rose gracefully, perched atop a long flaming column. It climbed vertically for 4.5 seconds and then began to tilt slightly, just as its designers had planned. Just

20 seconds after takeoff, the A-4 was traveling at a speed of 650 mph (1,046 km/hr)—nearly the speed of sound. A second later, an announcement came over the loudspeakers: "Sonic velocity!" The A-4 had just broken the sound barrier and was traveling faster than sound. Fifty-four seconds after takeoff, the rocket's fuel ran out. The A-4, which was now traveling close to 3,500 mph (5,630 km/hr), continued climbing.

Recalling this momentous occasion, Dornberger said, "For the first time in the history of the rocket, we had sent an automatically controlled rocket missile to the border of the atmosphere. . . and put it into practically airless space. We had been working 10 years for this day." Willy Ley was even more succinct. "Today the spaceship was born," he said.

In spite of this tremendous success, Nazi leader Adolf Hitler refused to continue supporting the work being done at Peenemünde. He was certain that he could win the war with conventional weapons and the new jet-propelled V-1—a small, pilotless airplane powered by an air-breathing pulse-jet engine. The "V" stood for "vergeltung," a German word meaning "vengeance."

Unlike the A-4, the V-1 burned ordinary fuel oil and didn't require dangerous, difficult-to-handle liquid oxygen. It was also cheaper and easier to manufacture than the A-4. But while the V-1 had some tremendous advantages, it also had some major drawbacks. It was so slow that enemy fighters could easily chase it and shoot it down. Also, it required an expensive, permanent launching site. (The A-4 could be fired from a portable launching stand.)

Eventually, Dornberger convinced Hitler to fund additional research on the A-4, which was now being referred to as the V-2. By this time, the war was beginning to go badly for Germany.

Because Hitler had now convinced himself that the V-2 would save Germany, he gave the project top priority. However, both Dornberger and von Braun knew that the V-2 would not be able to meet Hitler's expectations.

The Parts of a V-2 Rocket

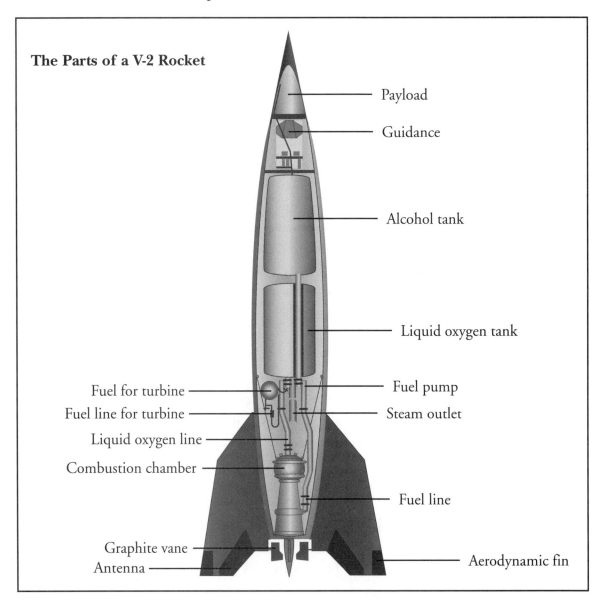

Payload

Guidance

Alcohol tank

Liquid oxygen tank

Fuel for turbine

Fuel pump

Fuel line for turbine

Steam outlet

Liquid oxygen line

Combustion chamber

Fuel line

Graphite vane

Antenna

Aerodynamic fin

A few months later, the British dropped 1,500 tons of explosives on Peenemünde, killing 800 people and nearly destroying the facility. Although only a few of the research and manufacturing buildings were damaged, research was halted for a month.

The Nazis were growing impatient. They insisted that the V-2 be put into full-scale production. Dornberger and von Braun knew that this was a bad decision; the V-2 wasn't ready. They had conducted only a few successful test flights and knew there were still design flaws to work out.

In the spring of 1944, the German secret police—the dreaded Gestapo—raided the Peenemünde facility and arrested a number of key scientists, including Wernher von Braun and Klaus Riedel. The Gestapo was jealous of the researchers' special status and frustrated by the secrecy surrounding the rocket facility. The Germans accused the scientists of sabotage and threatened them with execution. The Gestapo claimed that the researchers were working on rocket weapons only to accomplish their true goal—building a rocket that could travel in space. They accused Dornberger of intentionally delaying the development of the V-2.

Dornberger was concerned because the Gestapo was right. Although he had originally been interested in rockets only as weapons, the enthusiasm of von Braun and other scientists had won him over. He was captivated by the possibility of space travel. Dornberger dared not admit this, however. Instead, he vouched for the men's integrity and loyalty. He also pointed out that the execution of these men would spell disaster for the work at Peenemünde. The Gestapo, knowing that the V-2 was Hitler's pet project, realized they must allow the scientists to continue their work.

In September 1944, the first V-2s were launched across the English Channel. Before the end of the war, the Germans launched approximately 4,300 rockets at their enemies. More than 2,000 were aimed at the harbor at Antwerp, Belgium, which was an Allied stronghold. Another 1,500 were aimed at England. In most cases, London was the target. About 1,100 rockets hit British soil; the rest landed in the English Channel.

Like rockets used 200 years earlier, the success of the V-2 was the result of the number used. The Germans knew that if they launched enough rockets, some were bound to land on—or near—their target. In the end, the V-2 was never nearly as effective as Dornberger had hoped it would be. "It was a missile far short of what it could have been, a missile inadequate in accuracy and effect, which was exactly what we had anxiously striven for years to avoid, a weapon which, despite certain technical merits, was unequal to its task," he said.

The wartime use of the V-2 came to an end when Allied ground forces overwhelmed Peenemünde and the underground rocket factory near Niedersachswerfen. In order to keep papers and equipment from falling into the hands of the Soviet Union, the Americans and British took everything of value from Peenemünde and the other rocket research facilities. The Soviets were determined, however, not to go home empty-handed. They sent in several groups of scientists to determine what might be worth salvaging.

The Americans now had tons of documents and enough missile parts and equipment to assemble about 100 complete V-2 rockets. More importantly, they had more than 100 of the scientists who had designed and built these rockets. Among this group was Wernher von Braun. Von Braun had organized the group's surrender to the Americans because he thought the

United States could provide the resources required for inter-planetary travel. Von Braun, Dornberger, and the other scientists and engineers brought with them not just their knowledge and expertise, but a grand vision.

At that time, however, the United States government was far more interested in developing rocket weapons than spaceships. As it turned out, this was no great setback for the scientists. After all, a rocket is a rocket—the payload is interchangeable. The same rocket that launches an atomic bomb can also carry a person to the Moon.

When Peenemünde was captured by the Allies, Wehrner von Braun and many other scientists surrendered to the Americans. Later, von Braun contributed to a great deal to the American space program. This photograph was taken in his office at a space research center in Huntsville, Alabama in 1962.

6

PRELUDE TO SPACE

Robert Goddard died on August 10, 1945, just 4 days before the Japanese surrendered and World War II ended. Although he had continued to study rockets in his later years, Goddard had not shared any of his findings since his historic 1926 rocket launch. He explained his need for privacy and secrecy in a 1931 letter to the president of the American Rocket Society.

> It happens that so many of my ideas and suggestions have been copied abroad without the acknowledgment usual in scientific circles that I have been forced to take this attitude. Further, I do not think it desirable to publish results of the long series of experiments I have undertaken until I feel that I have made a significant further contribution to the problem.

Unfortunately, this secrecy forced groups like the ARS and the VfR to reinvent much of Goddard's work. According to one member of the ARS, "[Our first rocket designs were patterned] after one of the successful German liquid-fuel rockets [with] so many changes and inventions of our own that it must stand or fall upon its own merits." By the time Goddard's work became available, most of it had been duplicated—and even surpassed.

When Robert Goddard was shown one of the German V-2 rockets captured at Peenemünde, he was shocked. "I don't think he ever got over the V-2," a co-worker observed. "He felt the Germans had copied his work and that he could have produced a bigger, better, and less expensive rocket, if only the United States had accepted the long-range rocket." The German scientists claimed they had never seen any of Goddard's patents.

The U.S. Army, which was then in charge of the German scientists, began work exactly where the Germans had left off. After organizing tons of captured documents, the German scientists got to work. The first static test of a V-2 engine in the United States took place on March 14, 1946; the first flight was made a month later.

Although these initial tests involved German-made rockets, the German and American engineers were busy making improvements. A historic series of American V-2 launches began in 1948 with the start of Project Bumper. A WAC-Corporal, which was originally designed as a **sounding rocket**, was mounted in the nose of a V-2. When the V-2 reached its maximum altitude, the WAC-Corporal's engine was ignited. A rocket launched on February 24, 1949, reached a maximum height of 244 miles (393 km). No other rocket had ever gone so far. This was humanity's first tenuous step into space.

Meanwhile, the British were also thinking about ways to improve the V-2. In fact, British scientists were among the first to suggest modifying a V-2 so that a pilot could go on a suborbital flight—beyond Earth's atmosphere, but below the height

The first rocket launch from Cape Canaveral in Florida took place on July 24, 1950. The rocket—a V-2 first stage with a WAC-Corporal second stage—was propelled upward more than 200 miles (320 km).

necessary to **orbit** Earth. In 1946, H. E. Ross and R. A. Smith of the British Interplanetary Society (BIS) presented a design for a V-2 with a manned capsule. They called their vehicle *Megaroc*. Unfortunately, the British government refused to fund the project.

At about the same time, the RAND Corporation in the United States proposed an unmanned satellite launcher derived from the V-2. Like the BIS project, this too met with official indifference.

By 1950, the American V-2 was 5 feet (1.5 m) longer and could carry five times the payload of the original missile. Almost all the V-2s launched from the Army's test range in White Sands, New Mexico, were equipped with scientific instruments that collected and transmitted information about cosmic and solar radiation and micrometeorites, as well as the temperature, pressure, and composition of the atmosphere.

After the successes of the V-2 at White Sands, New Mexico, the Army moved its rocket development group to the Redstone Arsenal in Alabama, where the Army **Ballistic Missile** Agency (ABMA) was created. This group, under the direction of Major General John B. Medaris, designed and built the 58-foot (18-m)-tall Jupiter—America's first successful Intermediate Range Ballistic Missile (IRBM).

Meanwhile, the U.S. Navy was developing missiles of its own—such as the famous Polaris, Poseidon, and Viking missiles. These rockets could be fired from the decks of ships or submerged submarines. The Air Force developed the Atlas and Titan missiles. Although these rockets were designed for military use, the Jupiter, Atlas, and Titan eventually played significant roles in the history of spaceflight.

This Polaris missile was launched by the U.S. Navy on June 18, 1963.

The Soviet Union Uncovers German Secrets

The Soviets were also hard at work on new rocket designs. After the Americans and British left Peenemünde, the Soviets had discovered hidden caches containing V-2 rocket assemblies, tools, plans, and guidance equipment as well as storehouses full of spare parts. Because a few German scientists had chosen to turn themselves over to the Soviet Union rather than the United States or Great Britain, the Soviets now knew almost as much about rockets as the Americans. The German scientists in the Soviet Union established a new rocket research institute, which they called Rabe (an abbreviation for Russian words meaning "rocket manufacture and development"). Sergei Korolev was assigned to be Valentin Glushko's deputy and put in charge of the facility. By the fall of 1946, more than 5,000 scientists and technicians were working to produce flight-worthy V-2 rockets.

The first German-Soviet V-2 was called the R-1 (the "Pobeda," or "victory"). It was almost identical in size and outward appearance to the original German V-2, but it weighed a great deal more and had a new, more powerful engine.

Despite the Soviet emphasis on military rocket development, the Russian scientists were just as eager as their American counterparts to travel in space. The scientists continued improving and enlarging the R-1. The new rockets carried instruments—and even animals—up to 68 miles (109 km) above Earth's surface. Eventually, a second generation of R-1 rockets was developed. Using new materials and engines, this series of rockets was used well into the 1970s.

Sounding Rockets: A Closer Look

In 1936, Frank Malina, William Bollay, John Parsons, and Edward Forman established the GALCIT (Guggenheim Aeronautical Laboratory, California Institute of Technology) Rocket-Research Project. The goal of the project was to develop a solid- or liquid-fuel high-altitude sounding rocket—a rocket used to collect data about atmospheric conditions. Sounding rockets usually carry cameras, barometers, thermometers, and other scientific instruments.

By 1939, their work had attracted the attention of the Army Air Corps. The group received funding to work on jet-assisted take-off (JATO) units for aircraft. JATO rockets help heavily loaded airplanes lift off. America's first successful JATO unit was demonstrated in 1941. By 1942, the GALCIT project had evolved into a private company—Aerojet. In 1945, Aerojet developed the WAC-Corporal, a small liquid-fuel rocket. The WAC-Corporal was America's first operational sounding rocket. During its first test flight, the rocket climbed to an altitude of nearly 45 miles (72 km).

Aerojet's next project was the Aerobee, a liquid-fuel rocket with a small solid-fuel booster. It could carry up to 150 pounds (68 kg) of payload and climb more than 50 miles (80 km). The Aerobee was widely used until 1985, and evolved through several models. The final version could reach a height of 290 miles (467 km). The Aerobee took the first color photographs of Earth from space, collected micrometeoroids, and detected the first neutron stars.

Meanwhile, in 1946, the U.S. Navy and the Glenn L. Martin Company were developing a sounding rocket of their own. This rocket, the Viking, was larger and more powerful than the Aerobee. The

Viking, America's first large scale rocket, was 32 to 45 inches (81 to 114 cm) in diameter and about 46 feet (14 m) tall. In 1954, a Viking rocket set a single-stage rocket altitude record of 158 miles (254 km). However, because the Viking was so expensive to build and launch, only twelve were constructed.

The Deacon, a solid-fuel sounding rocket developed for the National Advisory Committee on Aeronautics (NACA), carried a 40-pound (18-kg) payload and cost only $4,000 to build.* Eventually, Deacon rockets were coupled with existing antiaircraft rockets to create a whole family of low-cost, reliable sounding rockets. These rockets could propel a 40-pound (18-kg) payload to an altitude of nearly 70 miles (113 km).

Because sounding rockets were not as glamorous as the rockets used to carry spacecraft with human passengers, it was more difficult to get funding for them. As a result, the designers were always looking for ways to cut the cost of producing them. One solution was to a use a balloon as a kind of first stage. The first "rockoons" launched a Deacon rocket from the deck of a Coast Guard ship. Once the rocket had reached a predetermined altitude, the rocket's engine was ignited by radio. Eighty-six rockoons were launched between July 1957 and December 1958.

A rockoon lifting off from a dock in San Diego, California. This first test flight was performed on October 3, 1956.

Other countries also developed sounding rockets. Between 1948 and 1950, the Soviets developed the "Meteo" rocket. With its solid fuel boosters, the Meteo could reach an altitude of 62 miles (100 km). Advanced Meteos were used well into the 1970s. The Soviets also had their big—75-foot (23-m) tall—Vertikal series, which was used between 1970 and 1981. The Vertikals had been developed from IRBM (Intermediate Range Ballistic Missile) nuclear missiles.

In 1950, the French began launching the Veronique, a rocket that former-German scientists had developed from the original V-2. It was so successful that it became the French equivalent of the American Aerobee and was used well into the 1970s.

Britain did not develop a sounding rocket of its own until 1956. The Skylark was designed by Walter Riedel, who had been von Braun's deputy at Peenemünde. More than 350 Skylarks have been launched to date. Later models, such as the three-stage Skylark 12, have carried 770-pound (349-kg) payloads as high as 620 miles (998 km).

In the mid-1950s, Japan developed tiny "pencil" rockets, which were just 9 to 12 inches (23 to 30 cm) long and less than 1 inch (2.5 cm) in diameter. Tiny as they were, these rockets provide valuable data on propellants and engine design. From the pencil rockets grew the Kappa series of solid-fuel rockets. In 1958, a Kappa 6 carried a 6-pound (2.7-kg) payload to an altitude of 135 miles (217 km). Eventually, the Japanese developed their highly successful Lambda series of four-stage sounding rockets.

Australia, India, Canada, Israel, and Brazil have also developed sounding rockets for scientific research.

---

*In 1958, the National Aeronautics and Space Administration (NASA) was created. It absorbed the National Advisory Committee on Aeronautics (NACA).

The International Geophysical Year

In 1952, the International Council of Scientific Unions (ICSU) proposed a unique international research project called the International Geophysical Year. Between July 1957 and December 1958, every corner of our planet and its atmosphere was thoroughly explored.

Because most of the atmospheric data would be collected by sounding rockets, both the United States and the Soviet Union knew that this was their chance to show the rest of the world that they were capable of great scientific and engineering achievements. In 1955, President Dwight Eisenhower announced that the United States would launch an Earth satellite as part of its "contribution" to the forthcoming International Geophysical Year. The Soviets, however, did not want to be left behind. They planned to launch an artificial satellite, too.* The Soviets knew that beating the Americans would be a great victory for Communism. The "Space Race" had begun. Over the years, it was to become a kind of bloodless war between the East and the West.

In the United States, scientists disagreed about what type of rocket should be used to launch its first satellite. The Navy's scientists wanted to build a specially designed **launch vehicle**—a rocket meant to boost another rocket, a **spaceplane**, a manned capsule, a space probe, or an artificial satellite. (A space probe is a spacecraft that carries research equipment on long voyages. An artificial satellite is a spacecraft intended to orbit Earth, the Moon, or another celestial body.)

* Human-made satellites are called "artificial" to distinguish them from natural satellites, such as moons. The word satellite is used to describe any object that orbits another body. The Moon is a satellite of Earth, and Earth is a satellite of the Sun.

Army scientists, led by von Braun, had a different idea. They wanted to modify the successful Jupiter rocket so that it could act as a launch vehicle. Although critics of the Navy's plan pointed out the enormous time and cost involved in developing an entirely new rocket, the United States decided to build a specially designed launch vehicle—the Vanguard.

Project Vanguard began on September 9, 1955, and by March 1956, a final design was approved. It was a handsome, three-stage rocket that looked like a slim, silvery needle. It was 72 feet (22 m) tall and only 45 inches (114 cm) in diameter. Although its first test flight was successful, the next two failed. One blew up on the launch pad; the other veered off course and broke apart when it was only 4 miles (6.4 km) high. The fourth launch was successful, but it was too late. The Soviets had already won the first battle of the Space Race. On October 4, 1957, they launched the first artificial satellite—*Sputnik 1.* *Sputnik's* beep-beep-beep signal was broadcast around the world.

This photo of Sputnik 1 *(mounted on a stand) was released to the foreign press on October 9, 1957—5 days after it was launched into space.*

The Americans were surprised and embarrassed when they heard the news. The scientists who had favored the Army's plan were furious. The Soviets had done just what von Braun suggested—modified a proven, reliable military rocket to carry a satellite. The Soviets had used the R-7, which was really a cluster of five ICBMs. The rocket was 33.7 feet (10.3 m) in diameter and nearly 96 feet (29 m) tall. It weighed about 588,735 pounds (267,048 kg), and its engines produced a combined thrust of more than 1.1 million pounds (498,956 kg). The R-7 was the largest, most powerful rocket in the world.

After the combined humiliation of Vanguard's failure and *Sputnik's* success, von Braun again urged the U.S. government to let him go ahead with his plan. The Army claimed that they could get a satellite up in just 4 months at a cost of $12,750,000—a fraction of the cost of the Vanguard program. Three weeks after the launch of *Sputnik 1*, ABMA got the go-ahead and a deadline of January 30, 1958—barely 3 months! The Vanguard project had taken more than 2.5 years.*

In that short time, von Braun and his team built six launch vehicles, and they launched *Explorer 1*, America's first Earth satellite, on January 31, 1958. The team was only 1 day behind schedule. The United States swore it would never again come in second in the Space Race.

The United States had learned a hard lesson. From that point on, American scientists took an evolutionary approach to rocket design. They used past, successful rockets as a starting point, instead of creating new, unproven designs. An entirely new, designed-from-scratch American space rocket was not built until the 1980s.

---

* Vanguard finally propelled its first satellite about 6 weeks after *Explorer 1* was launched.

Launch Vehicles: A Closer Look

Since the mid-1950s, when the R-7 and the Vanguard were developed, the United States, the Soviet Union, and several other nations have produced a variety of launch vehicles. Although the United States abandoned Vanguard, it went on to design and build many other launch vehicles based on rockets originally developed as military ballistic missiles. As you will learn in Chapter 7, the Atlas launch vehicle propelled the first American into Earth orbit as part of the Mercury program; the Titan powered the Gemini spacecraft; and the mighty Saturn carried the Apollo spacecraft and human beings to the Moon.

A larger, more powerful version of the Titan was later used to place heavy satellites in orbit. Titan launch vehicles also propelled the two Viking probes to the planet Mars and the two Voyager probes to the outer solar system.

The first Delta launch vehicle was 8 feet (2.4 m) in diameter and stood 91 feet (28 m) high. Its first successful launch—in 1960—put a satellite called *Echo 1* into orbit.

Rockets that participated in the American manned space program

Mercury Atlas   Gemini-Titan II   Saturn 5

Echo was little more than an enormous silver balloon that could be seen from the ground and was used for navigation. Over the next three decades, thirteen more Delta rockets were built. The first of these could place a 100-pound (45-kg) satellite into a low Earth orbit —about 100 to 500 miles (161 to 805 km) above Earth—while the final model was able to place a 2,292-pound (1,040-kg) satellite into a geosynchronous orbit— 12,000 miles (19,300 km) above Earth's surface. Delta rockets carried dozens of satellites into orbit. These satellites help people all over the world to communicate, predict the weather, and perform scientific investigations.

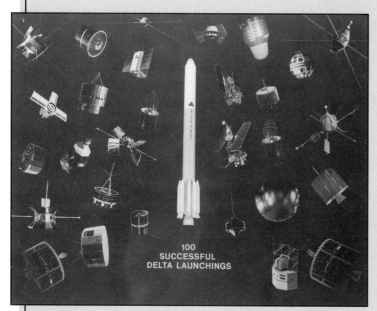

After its introduction in 1960, the Delta launch vehicle was used extensively by the United States to transport all kinds of satellites into space. This illustrations shows just some of the payloads propelled into Earth orbit by the Delta.

The Scout, a low-cost launch vehicle, was first used in 1960. Although it was originally designed to place 150-pound (68-kg) satellites into 300-mile (483-km) orbits, the three-stage 72-foot (22-m)-long Scout gradually evolved into a larger, more powerful, and more useful rocket. Scouts have launched more than 100 satellites, including many built outside the United States. By 1989, Scout rockets were capable of carrying 450-pound (204-kg) satellites to an orbit 300 miles (483 km) above Earth.

For more than 30 years, the Soviets relied on the R-7 to boost most of their satellites. In 1965, the Soviets also began to use the Proton, which was designed by Sergei Korolev to place heavy satellite loads into Earth orbit. The Proton rockets ranged in height from 171 to 195 feet (52 to 59 m) and were about 30 feet (9 m) in diameter. In recent years, the Proton has been used to launch satellites for other nations.

The United States and the Soviet Union weren't the only countries that wanted to get into space. Many European nations were anxious to develop their own launch vehicles, mainly because both the United States and the Soviet Union were charging other countries very large fees to launch satellites. Any country that could develop its own rockets could save that money and also get a piece of the lucrative launch market.

Since few countries possess the enormous financial and industrial resources of the United States or the former Soviet Union, the European nations banded together in 1962 to form the European Launcher Development Organization (ELDO), headquartered in Paris. The group's first spacecraft was the *Europa 1*. It had a British first stage, a French second stage, and a German third stage.

In 1974, ELDO changed its name to the European Space Agency (ESA). The organization continued to work toward developing a satellite launch vehicle. The Ariane, which was first launched in 1979, quickly racked up a long list of impressive achievements. It began commercial service in 1984 when the first private American satellite was launched on a non-American launch vehicle. The Ariane 3 consists of a Viking first and second stage plus two Italian-made strap-on solid-fuel boosters. The Ariane 4, introduced in 1988, is almost twice as powerful as its predecessor. It is capable of sending 9,000-pound (4,082-kg) payloads into geosynchronous orbit.

A special launch site was built for the Ariane rocket in French Guiana, which lies on the northeast coast of South America. The location was chosen partly because it is on French soil, but mainly because it is only 5 degrees from the equator. Earth spins at a rate of 1,000 mph (1,609 km/hr) at the equator. A rocket launched in the direction of this spin will pick up that extra 1,000 mph (1,609 km/hr). (Kennedy Space Center was chosen as the primary American launch facility for the same reason. Florida is closer to the equator than any other part of the continental United States.)

The Europeans were not the only ones eager to have their own space program. Japan, which had long wanted its own launch vehicle so that it could compete with the United States for commercial satellite contracts, did something very unusual. The Japanese established two entirely different space agencies—the National Space Development Agency (NASDA) and the Institute for Space and Astronautical Sciences (ISAS). NASDA deals with the commercial applications of space, while ISAS deals with the scientific aspects. Beginning with launch vehicles purchased from the United States, Japan eventually developed its own line of successful rockets.

In 1972, a 77.4-foot (23.6-m) Mu rocket carried Japan's second satellite into orbit. Modified versions of the Mu were used until 1975, when Japan switched to liquid-fuel N-class rockets. The original models of this launcher used a version of the American Delta booster as their first stage. A later version of this rocket, called the N-2, carried Japan's first deep-space probes to Halley's Comet.

Although France is a member of ESA, it also founded its own space program in 1962, and has built a number of expendable vehicle launchers. The most successful of these is the Diamant series.

7

ROCKET RIDERS

However advanced military rockets may have become, however exciting it might have been to put unmanned satellites into orbit, the ultimate goal of rocket scientists and engineers never changed. They wanted to launch a human being into space. Everything else was just preliminary.

Traveling into space was something humans had dreamed of for centuries. In 1913, a stuntman named F. Rodman Law built an enormous skyrocket 10 feet (3 m) long and 4 feet (1.2 m) in diameter. It was balanced with a 20-foot (6-m)-long piece of heavy timber. Law hoped to soar 3,500 feet (1,067 m) into the air and land 12 miles (19 km) away by parachute. Law's rocket exploded, but he survived.

On June 11, 1928, German pilot Friedrich Stamer took off in a rocket-propelled glider that he had developed with Max Valier and Fritz von Opel. As you learned earlier, Valier was a pioneer promoter and popularizer of rocket flight as well as a founding member of the VfR, and Opel was a wealthy automobile manu-facturer who financed many rocket experiments. The aircraft that Stamer flew was a specially adapted glider called the *Ente*, which means "duck" in German. It was propelled by two powerful solid-fuel rockets built in a factory Stamer owned. The flight lasted less than 2 minutes.

The Rise of Rocket-Powered Aircraft

After this triumph, many other European inventors, adventurers, and pilots built and flew their own rocket-powered aircraft. Some of these aircraft, such as the one flown by Gottlob Espenlaub, were quite advanced and very successful. The first American to fly a rocket-powered aircraft was William Swan, who took off from Atlantic City, New Jersey, in 1934.

Most early rocket-propelled aircraft were designed and built by amateurs. All this changed during World War II. The Messerschmidt Me-163 *Komet*—a stumpy, delta-winged fighter was the most famous rocket-powered aircraft used in combat. It could fly more than 600 mph (966 km/hr), which is close to the speed of sound.

Wernher von Braun and his colleagues at Peenemünde also hoped to combine rockets in order to reach greater heights. The A-9 would have had slender wings and landing gear, so that it could return to its base after dropping a bomb. The A-10, which would have been 65 feet (20 m) tall and more than 13 feet (4 m) in diameter, could have carried the A-9 in its nose, just as the Bumper Project's V-2 carried a WAC-Corporal missile.

In 1944, the United States National Advisory Committee for Astronautics (NACA) announced plans to develop a single-pilot rocket plane that could travel faster than sound. This effort, which became the Air Force's X-1 program, was undertaken by Bell Aircraft. The scientists and engineers at Bell Aircraft designed a small, sleek, bullet-shaped aircraft.* Since it could not carry enough fuel to get off the ground, engineers intended to drop the X-1 from another aircraft. The bomb bay of a B-29 bomber was modified to hold the rocket plane.

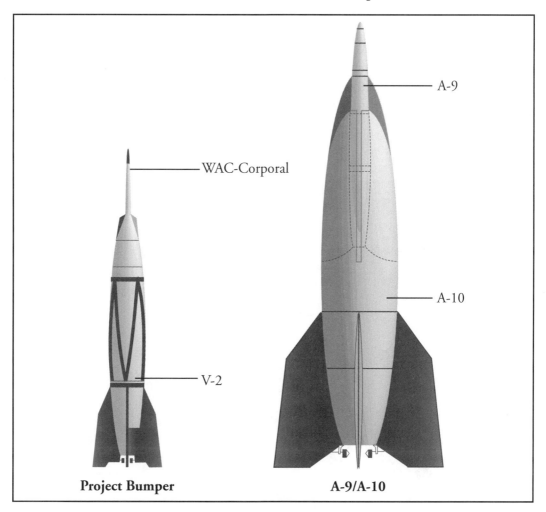

Project Bumper   **A-9/A-10**

The rocket combination used as part of Project Bumper was very similar to German plans to combine the A-9 and A-10 rockets.

*The bullet shape of the X-1 was no coincidence. It was intentionally designed to resemble a .50-caliber bullet.

The first tests began in 1946. On October 14, 1947, X-1 pilot Captain Charles Yaeger of the U.S. Air Force became the first person to travel faster than the speed of sound. By 1949, the X-1 could travel 970 mph (1,561 km/hr) and reach an altitude of 14 miles (23 km).

The U.S. Navy, meanwhile, had been experimenting with its own rocket plane—a beautiful white aircraft called the D-558-2, or the *Skyrocket.* It was the first aircraft to fly at twice the speed of sound. It used the same four-chambered Reaction Motors rocket engine as the X-1. Because it was difficult for the pilots to control the thrust of this rocket motor, they adjusted their

The Air Force's X-1 program developed a series of rocket planes, such as the one pictured here, that could fly faster than the speed of sound.

speed by turning different combinations of the motor's four chambers on or off. (Each of these chambers could produce 1,500 pounds [680 kg] of thrust.)

The success of these experiments encouraged NACA to be even more ambitious. In 1953, the organization recommended that researchers address "the problems of manned flight at altitudes between 12 and 50 miles (19 to 80 km) and at speeds of **Mach** 4 through 10." The aircraft that accomplished these goals was the X-15, which many people consider the world's first true spaceship. It was ready for test flights in 1960.

Many people consider the X-15 the world's first spaceship because it could reach altitudes greater than 50 miles (80 km)—the point where Earth's atmosphere ends and space begins.

In 1963, the X-15 set an unofficial altitude record of 67 miles (108 km)—high enough to qualify as space. Because of flights like these, many of the X-15 pilots are considered astronauts. By 1966, the X-15 had flown faster than Mach 3 (three times the speed of sound) for more than 4 hours; faster than Mach 4 for more than 2.5 hours; faster than Mach 5 for more than 40 minutes; and faster than Mach 6 for 12 seconds. In 1967, the X-15 reached Mach 6.7.

The X-15 made a total of 199 flights. The data collected during these flights were used to design more advanced spacecraft. For this reason, the X-15 is considered one of the most successful experimental aircraft in history. The X-15's achievements were so spectacular that scientists thought about putting it into orbit. This idea did not get far, however. By this time, interest in rocket aircraft was dwindling.

From Aircraft to Spacecraft

Instead of developing a spacecraft that could take off, fly into orbit, and then return as a glider, American scientists and engineers developed spacecraft that would be powered by rockets that were originally designed as military ballistic missiles.

A ballistic missile is a type of guided missile. During the first part of its flight, the missile's rocket engine propels it to a planned flight path. When the ballistic missile is on course, its engine shuts off. The missile coasts through the second part of its flight and then free-falls until it hits its target—if it is being used to carry a warhead—or is destroyed while still in the air—after boosting a spacecraft.

On May 5, 1961, Commander Alan B. Shepard became the first American to be launched into space. His Mercury spacecraft was launched with the Redstone launch vehicle, which was very similar to the modified Jupiter rocket that had launched

Explorer 1. Because this rocket was not powerful enough to put Shepard's 3,200-pound (1,450-kg) Mercury capsule into orbit, Shepard made a suborbital flight that took him 116.5 miles (187.5 km) above Earth's surface. Two months later, Major Virgil (Gus) Grissom made a nearly identical flight.

The first American to achieve Earth orbit was Colonel John H. Glenn, Jr. Glenn's Mercury capsule was launched by a giant Atlas missile, which had originally been designed to carry heavy nuclear weapons. It had no problem putting a manned capsule into orbit.

Mercury-Atlas 6 with John Glenn aboard lifts off from Cape Canaveral in Florida (left). A close-up view of the Mercury capsule (right).

Project Mercury: A Closer Look

Mission	Astronaut	Launch Date
Mercury-Redstone 3	Shepard	May 5, 1961
Mercury-Redstone 4	Grissom	July 21, 1961
Mercury-Atlas 6	Glenn	February 20, 1962
Mercury-Atlas 7	Carpenter	May 24, 1962
Mercury-Atlas 8	Schirra	October 3, 1962
Mercury-Atlas 9	Cooper	May 15, 1963

While these missions were tremendous accomplishments, they did not thrill Americans as much as they might have because the Soviet Union had beaten the United States again. On April 12, 1961—almost a month before Alan Shepard's sub-orbital flight—the Soviets launched the first human being into space. Because they used a more powerful rocket than the Redstone launch vehicle, the Soviet's 5-ton *Vostok* (the Russian word for "east") spacecraft with Major Yuri Gagarin on board made one orbit around Earth.

The Americans were sick and tired of being shown up by the Soviets. After another three successful Mercury flights, U.S.

On April 12, 1961, cosmonaut Yuri Gagarin became the first human being launched into space.

scientists began designing a larger capsule that could carry two or more astronauts. But once again, the Soviets beat the Americans. On October 12, 1964, three Soviet cosmonauts went into orbit. Their spacecraft, the *Voskhod 1* (the Russian word for "sunrise") was incredibly advanced. It weighed almost 6 tons, making it the largest object ever launched into space.

In March 1965, just 5 months later, the Soviets accomplished an even greater feat. One of the two crew members of *Voskhod 2*, Lieutenant Colonel Alexei A. Leonov, left the spacecraft through an airlock and became the first person to walk in space.

Meanwhile, the Americans had begun Project Gemini.* The Gemini capsule was entirely different from the Mercury. It was more or less the same shape, but it weighed 2.5 times as much. It also had controls that allowed the astronauts to change the vehicle's orbit. This feature made it a true spacecraft. The Gemini capsules were launched by a Titan 2 ballistic missile.

On March 23, 1965, 5 days after the *Voskhod 2* flight, the first manned Gemini flight—*Gemini 3*—took Gus Grissom and Lieutenant Commander John W. Young into space. Three months later, on the *Gemini IV* flight, Edward H. White left the spacecraft for the first American space walk. He drifted a considerable distance away from the capsule, tethered only by his life-support hose.

Although some of the twelve flights in the Gemini program had problems, they accomplished many important goals—space-walking, the rendezvous and docking of two orbiting

* The Gemini spacecraft carried two astronauts and was named after the zodiac constellation, which is supposed to represent twins. *Gemini 1* and *2* carried no human passengers.

spacecraft (*Gemini VIII* and an unmanned Agena vehicle), the study of prolonged weightlessness, and improved landing techniques. The Americans knew that the next step was the Apollo mission—manned flights to the Moon.

A Gemini spacecraft takes off from Cape Kennedy (formerly Cape Canaveral) in Florida (bottom left). A close-up view of the Gemini capsule (top right).

Project Gemini: A Closer Look

Gemini 3
Grissom (left) and
Young (right)

Gemini VI
Stafford (left) and
Schirra (right)

Gemini V
Cooper (left) and
Conrad (right)

Mission	Astronauts	Launch Date
Gemini 3*	Grissom and Young	March 23, 1965
Gemini IV	McDivitt and White	June 3, 1965
Gemini V	Cooper and Conrad	August 21, 1965
Gemini VII	Borman and Lovell	December 4, 1965
Gemini VI	Stafford and Schirra	December 15, 1965
Gemini VIII	Armstrong and Scott	March 16, 1966
Gemini IX	Stafford and Cernan	June 3, 1966
Gemini X	Young and Collins	July 18, 1966
Gemini XI	Conrad and Gordon	September 12, 1966
Gemini XII	Lovell and Aldrin	November 11, 1966

* The use of Roman numerals for missions began with Gemini IV.

From Earth to the Moon

Project Apollo was officially announced on July 29, 1960. The spacecraft were to be propelled by a Saturn rocket booster. Work on the Saturn had begun in the late 1950s under the direction of Wernher von Braun. Even then, von Braun had realized that boosters based on ICBMs were nowhere near powerful enough to propel a spacecraft to the Moon. Rather than invent an entirely new super-booster, he proposed basing the new rocket design on existing, proven technology—such as that of the Redstone and its cousin, the Jupiter.

The first Saturn rocket, the Saturn C-1, was 162 feet (49 m) tall and weighed nearly 1 million pounds (453,597 kg). It consisted of a cluster of eight Redstone fuel tanks around a Jupiter tank. These tanks fueled eight upgraded Jupiter rocket engines. The rocket's upper stages varied depending on the specific requirements of each mission. When the Saturn C-1 was test-launched on October 27, 1961, it made a successful suborbital flight. After a few more tests, the Saturn C-1 was put into orbit.

Following this success, scientists began working on an even larger rocket—the Saturn 1B. It was 224 feet (68 m) tall, 21.7 feet (6.6 m) in diameter and weighed 650 tons when it was fully fueled and loaded. The Saturn 1B made its first suborbital flight on February 26, 1966, with an unmanned Apollo spacecraft as payload. Meanwhile, another group of scientists was building Saturn 5—the rocket that eventually propelled three astronauts to the Moon.

The Saturn 5 was a monster. It was 363 feet (111 m) tall—more than forty stories high. Fully fueled and loaded, it weighed more than 6 million pounds (2.7 million kg). It was a three-stage rocket, and each stage had its own name and manufacturer.

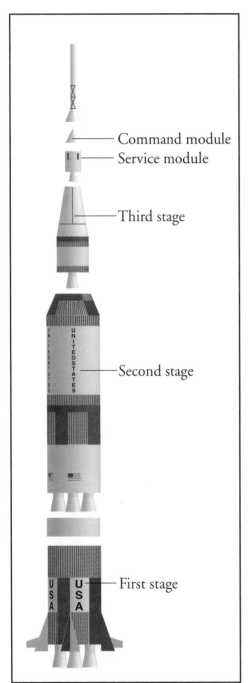

Command module

Service module

Third stage

Second stage

First stage

The first stage, the S-1C, was built by the Boeing Company. It was 138 feet (42 m) tall and 33 feet (10 m) in diameter. It weighed nearly 300,000 pounds (136,100 kg) empty, and could hold about 4.7 million pounds (2.1 million kg) of fuel and oxidizer (kerosene and liquid oxygen). This stage was powered by five enormous F-1 engines; each engine could produce 1.5 million pounds (680,395 kg) of thrust. The second stage, the S-2, was built by North American Aviation. It was 81.5 feet (25 m) tall and 33 feet (10 m) in diameter. It was powered by five smaller J-2 engines that together produced 1,164,000 pounds (527,980 kg) of thrust. The final stage, the S-4B, was 58.1 feet (18 m) tall and 21.7 feet (6.6 m) in diameter. It had a single J-2 engine.

The assembly of this enormous rocket required the largest building in the world. The transport crawler that carried

The Saturn 5 had three stages. The first and second stages launched the Apollo spacecraft into space. The third stage put the spacecraft into orbit around Earth and then on course to the Moon. The Apollo spacecraft consisted of a command module, a service module, and a lunar module.

the fully assembled rocket to its launch site took 10 hours to travel just 3 miles (4.8 km). Special barges were constructed to deliver the three stages from their manufacturers. Building the Saturn 5 took 5 years and the efforts of more than 325,000 people working for 12,000 different companies. It was the largest, most complex, and most powerful rocket ever built.

At the very top of this huge rocket booster was its payload:

• the Apollo command module, a gumdrop-shaped capsule that would carry the three Apollo astronauts to lunar orbit and then back to Earth;

• the cylindrical Apollo service module, which contained life support, propulsion, electrical, and other systems;

• the Apollo lunar module, which resembled a wind-up toy more than a spaceship.

Apollo 1 was never officially launched. During a routine test a week before the scheduled launch, astronauts Gus Grissom, Ed White, and Roger Chaffee died in a flash fire that raged through the interior of the Command Module. Discovering the cause of the fire and correcting the problem set the space program back nearly 2 years.

It was not until the launch of *Apollo 7* on October 11, 1968, that human beings were finally carried into space atop a Saturn booster. Once in Earth orbit, flight commander Wally Schirra performed a perfect practice rendezvous with the Saturn 5's spent second stage, which had followed the Command Module into orbit.

Apollo 8 carried astronauts beyond the orbit of Earth for the first time. On Christmas Day in 1968, astronauts Frank Borman, Jim Lovell, and William Anders flew to the Moon, orbited it 10 times, and then returned to Earth.

All of the Apollo spacecraft were launched from Cape Kennedy in Florida (bottom right). The Apollo 9 *capsule with James A. McDivitt, David R. Scott, and Russell L. Schweickart landed safely in the Atlantic Ocean (top left).*

Apollo 9 was an Earth orbit flight that tested the ungainly Lunar Module. Like Apollo 8, *Apollo 10* carried three men to the Moon. The difference was that, this time, two of the astronauts—Tom Stafford and Gene Cernan—rode to within 9 miles (14.5 km) of the lunar surface in the Lunar Module. The temptation to land must have been tremendous! Because the spacecraft performed flawlessly, NASA decided that the next flight—*Apollo 11*—would land on the moon.

Project Apollo: A Closer Look

Apollo 11
Armstrong (left),
Collins (center),
Aldrin (right)

Apollo 7
Cunningham (left),
Schirra (center),
Eisel (right)

Apollo 13
Lovell (left),
Swigert (center),
Haise (right)

Mission	Astronauts	Launch Date
Apollo 7	Cunningham, Schirra, Eisel	October 11, 1968
Apollo 8	Borman, Lovell, Anders	December 21, 1968
Apollo 9	McDivitt, Scott, Schweickart	March 3, 1969
Apollo 10	Stafford, Young, Cernan	May 18, 1969
Apollo 11	Armstrong, Collins, Aldrin	July 16, 1969
Apollo 12	Conrad, Gordon, Bean	November 14, 1969
Apollo 13	Lovell, Swigert, Haise	April 11, 1970
Apollo 14	Shepard, Roosa, Mitchell	January 31, 1971
Apollo 15	Scott, Worden, Irwin	July 26, 1971
Apollo 16	Young, Mattingly, Duke	April 16, 1972
Apollo 17	Cernan, Evans, Schmitt	December 7, 1972

Apollo 11 was launched on July 16, 1969, carrying Neil Armstrong, Edward E. (Buzz) Aldrin, and capsule commander Michael Collins. Four days later, Armstrong and Aldrin stepped from the Lunar Module onto the surface of the Moon. They were the first human beings to walk on another world.

Only six more Apollo flights followed. All of them, except the infamous *Apollo 13*, were enormous successes. With the return of *Apollo 17*, the United States abandoned its lunar landing program and the mighty Saturn 5 never flew again.

The Soviets Lose Their Edge

Meanwhile, the unbroken string of Soviet successes came to an end. In 1967, the first flight of their new *Soyuz* (the Russian word for "union") spacecraft had a tragic ending. The capsule's parachute system failed and the spacecraft crashed after re-entry, killing the cosmonaut on board. It was a year and a half before the Soviets launched another spacecraft.

In April 1971, the *Soyuz 10* docked with a previously launched space laboratory. Together they formed *Salyut 1* (the Russian word for "Salute"), the world's first space station. Two months later, three more cosmonauts died. After spending 24 days onboard *Salyut*, the three died as they were returning to Earth when air leaked out of their *Soyuz 11* spacecraft.

While the United States was garnering triumph after triumph in the Apollo program, the Soviets continued to stoutly deny any interest in manned lunar landings. Only in recent years has the rest of the world discovered that the Soviet Union was actually very interested in landing cosmonauts on the Moon. In fact, the Soviets had an active lunar landing program underway when the United States was developing Apollo.

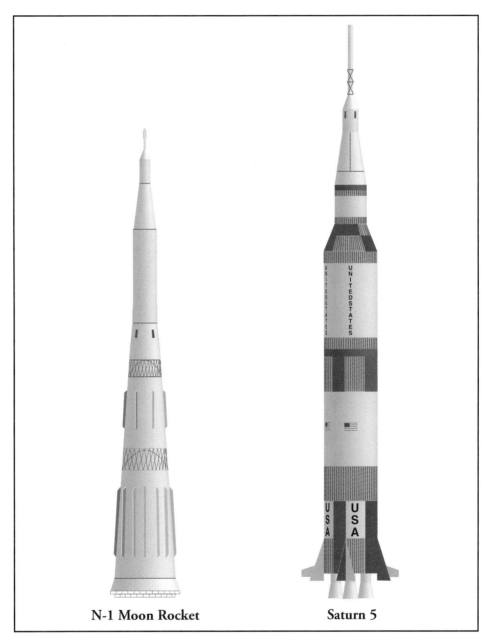

N-1 Moon Rocket   **Saturn 5**

The Soviets planned to send cosmonauts to the Moon using an N-1 Moon Rocket, but canceled the project in 1968.

In 1961, Chief Designer Sergei Korolev began to develop the giant N-1 booster, the Soviet equivalent of the Saturn 5. According to the plans, the three-stage Soviet rocket was almost exactly the same height as the American booster. The first stage of the Soviet booster had 30 engines that produced a combined thrust of 10.1 million pounds (4.6 million kg). The second stage had 8 engines, and the third had 4 engines.

The N-1 booster would carry the lunar spacecraft—a single-engined fourth stage, a lunar lander, and a command module—into orbit. The lander was designed to carry a single cosmonaut to the surface of the Moon and back into lunar orbit. The mission was originally scheduled for the end of 1968—nearly a year before the American landing. Due to limited funding and three N-1 explosions, however, the Soviet initiative to carry cosmonauts to the Moon was canceled.

8

SPACE SHUTTLES

Can you imagine buying a new bicycle every time you wanted to go somewhere? Just think about how much that would cost! The very idea seems ridiculous, doesn't it? Yet, that's exactly what the Soviet and American space programs did for decades. Each of the giant boosters and the capsules they carried were used only once and then discarded. Each of these rockets cost millions of dollars to build. In the United States, all that money came out of taxpayers' pockets. Rocket scientists knew it was time to design boosters and spacecraft that could be reused.

The idea of reusable spacecraft was certainly not new. During World War II, Eugen Sänger and Irene Bredt designed the *Silver Bird* **antipodal** bomber—a streamlined, winged spaceplane that would be launched from a long horizontal track. A booster would accelerate the bomber to a speed of 1,000 mph (1,609 km/hr), and the bomber would then continue under its own power. When the bomber passed over its target, it would drop a bomb and then continue around the world and land where it had taken off. Although the *Silver Bird* never got off the drawing board, it laid the groundwork for many future spaceplane designs, including today's space shuttles.

97

In the mid-1950s, Wernher von Braun published a series of articles in *Collier's* magazine. This series was so important that it is often referred to as "the *Collier's* Space Program." In one article, von Braun proposed a giant three-stage ferry rocket. The first two stages would return to Earth by parachute, and be used again. The third stage was a winged aircraft that would deliver its cargo into orbit and then re-enter Earth's atmosphere and land like a conventional airplane.

The X-20 Dyna-Soar *project was canceled in 1963.*

At about the same time that the X-15 was flying, the Air Force was developing a reusable spaceplane called the X-20 *Dyna-Soar* (short for "dynamic soaring"). *The Dyna-Soar* was a two-passenger winged spacecraft that could carry cargo and humans into orbit. According to the plans, it would be sent into space atop a Titan launch vehicle. Due to a lack of interest and funding, however, the project was canceled in 1963. Even today, many people think that the United States should have proceeded with the *Dyna-Soar*, rather than the Mercury program.

Toward the end of the Apollo program it became obvious that the United States needed a "space truck" that could carry cargo and passengers into orbit and then return to Earth for another trip. During the late 1960s and early 1970s, scientists and engineers at NASA studied dozens of designs for reusable space shuttles. By the late 1960s, NASA officials had decided that their Space Shuttle should be a two-stage rocket consisting of a fully reusable orbiter and a fully reusable booster. In most of the preliminary designs, both the orbiter and the booster were winged rockets. Each component had a pilot and crew that would land it like a regular aircraft.

At about this time, however, Congress began cutting NASA's budget. As a result, NASA had to sacrifice some of the shuttle's reusable features. First, they abandoned the idea of the fly-back booster. To decrease the size of the orbiter, the designers moved its fuel from internal tanks to disposable drop tanks. Next, they decided that the oxidizer would also go in an external dispos-able tank. When the new designs were finished, NASA was left with a partially reusable spacecraft that really didn't satisfy any-one. The orbiter and the solid-fuel boosters can be recycled, but the giant external fuel tank is discarded during each flight.

The Space Shuttle orbiter is 122 feet (37 m) long, with a wingspan of 78 feet (24 m). Its cargo bay is 15 feet (4.5 m) wide and 60 feet (18 m) long. It has a two-level control cabin. The liv-ing quarters are on the lower deck and the flight deck is on the upper level. The orbiter has three main engines, each capable of producing 375,000 pounds (170,000 kg) of thrust. The engines burn liquid hydrogen and liquid oxygen, so the exhaust consists of superheated steam! Smaller auxiliary engines that burn hydrazine and nitrogen tetroxide give the orbiter its final push into orbit.

The first flights of the shuttle orbiter were unpowered glider tests. It was released from a piggyback position on top of a specially adapted 747 airplane. After these trials and many static tests of the boosters and main engines, the Space Shuttle was ready for its first orbital launch.

The first Space Shuttle, the *Columbia*, was joined to its boosters and external tank on December 26, 1980. After 3 months of tests and checks, the Shuttle was ready for launch on April 10, 1981. More than 2,000 reporters and 300,000 spectators gathered to watch the historic event. Some minor problems delayed the launch for 2 days, so *Columbia* ended up taking off on the twentieth anniversary of Yuri Gagarin's first trip into orbit! The *Columbia* carried pilot John Young, copilot Robert Crippen, and an array of instruments that would record every detail of the shuttle's behavior.

At 7:00 A.M., on April 12, the world's first reusable spaceship lifted off a launch pad at Kennedy Space Center in Florida. It was the eightieth manned spaceflight and the seventy-seventh vehicle to achieve Earth orbit. Less than 10 minutes after take-

The Space Shuttle Columbia *touched down at Edward's Air Force Base in California on April 14, 1981.*

off, the shuttle was in orbit 170 miles (274 km) above Earth. Two days later, the *Columbia* returned to Earth, landing at Edwards Air Force Base in California. The mission had been a tremendous success.

The first flight of the *Columbia* (STS 1) was followed by three more test flights. The astronauts on STS 3 tested the remote manipulator arm, which has since become an invaluable tool. The first fully operational flight of the shuttle was STS 5. The orbiter carried scientific experiments and launched a satellite. In addition, a space walk was performed inside the payload bay by astronauts Story Musgrave and Donald Peterson. The seventh shuttle flight, which launched in June 1983, carried Sally K. Ride, the first female American astronaut, into orbit. Twenty years earlier, Soviet cosmonaut Valentina Tereshkova had become the first woman in space.

Soon the Space Shuttle fleet included three new shuttles—*Atlantis*, *Discovery*, and *Challenger*. The Space Shuttle proved so successful that its launches and landings quickly became almost as routine as the scheduled flights of an ordinary airline. This was extremely frustrating to people who were trying to promote and increase public interest in space travel. Spaceflight had become an ordinary, everyday experience rather than an exciting event. Space Shuttle launches seldom made front-page news, and Russian launches were often not mentioned at all.

Ironically, this indifference was exactly what space travel enthusiasts had always been working toward. The history of aviation offers a good analogy. Back in the 1920s and 1930s there was a "golden age" of aviation—everyone was interested and excited about flying. Records were being made and broken every day and famous pilots were household names. Sixty years ago, every flight across the Atlantic Ocean rated headlines in newspapers across the country. Today, hundreds of airplanes carry thousands of passengers from the United States to Europe and back again. Some of these people fly in the Concorde, which travels faster than the speed of sound. No one gives these flights a second thought. Can you even imagine every airline flight from New York to Paris getting a headline?

The same thing began to happen to spaceflight. It had become so safe, so predictable, so repetitive that it no longer excited or interested the general public. This changed on January 28, 1986, when the Space Shuttle *Challenger* exploded, killing all seven people on board. It was a very cold day, and the low temperature had damaged the O-rings on the solid fuel boosters. The O-rings are seals that keep the intense blast contained inside the boosters. Several engineers had expressed concern about launching when the weather was so cold, but they were ignored.

Just 1 second after liftoff, steam and black smoke began to leak from a joint in one of the boosters. A few seconds later, flames shot from the seam and hit the side of the external fuel tank like a blowtorch. The link between the booster and the fuel tank was burned through, and the flaming booster rocket swung free. The giant fuel tank ruptured, and broke off part of *Challenger's* wing. The thousands of tons of hydrogen and oxygen in the tank erupted almost instantly, engulfing the spacecraft in an enormous explosion. Thrown free, the orbiter tumbled wildly. Within seconds, it disintegrated.

This was the first American mission to involve in-flight fatalities. It came as a tremendous shock to a nation that had begun to take its space program for granted. It was also a major blow to American prestige and an embarrassment to NASA, especially when the investigation that followed showed that much of the fault lay with NASA officials.

The Space Shuttle Challenger *explosion on January 28, 1986 stunned most Americans.*

The Space Shuttle program was put on hold for 2 years while the spacecraft was redesigned and NASA examined its procedures. NASA scientists and engineers made countless modifications to the spacecraft and the main engines. An escape system was also added for the crew. The first launch with the redesigned spacecraft *Discovery* went just as planned. Since that time, there have been more than fifty successful Space Shuttle flights.

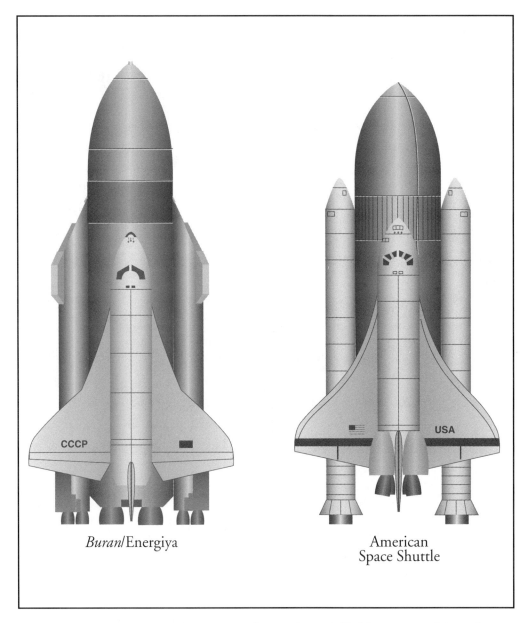

Buran/Energiya   American
                         Space Shuttle

The Soviet space shuttle consists of an orbiter called **Buran** *and a rocket booster called Energiya. It is very similar to the American Space Shuttle, which consists of an orbiter, two booster rockets, and an external fuel tank.*

The Soviet Space Shuttle

In the late 1980s, the Soviet Union developed its own space shuttle—the VKK *Buran* (meaning Air-Spacecraft *Snowstorm*). The *Buran* is slightly larger than the American Space Shuttle. It has a wingspan of 79 feet (24 m) and is 118 feet (36 m) long. Like the Space Shuttle, it has a two-deck crew compartment that can accommodate two to four cosmonauts and six passengers. Its maximum launching weight is 105 tons, and it can carry 30 tons into orbit.

The biggest difference between *Buran* and the Space Shuttle is not in the orbiter, but in the method used to launch it. While the American spacecraft uses strap-on solid-fuel boosters and an external fuel tank, the *Buran* is lifted by a single, enormous liquid-fuel booster rocket called the Energiya (a Russian word meaning energy). Since *Buran* doesn't need big main engines to lift itself into orbit, it has only small engines that are used for orbital maneuvering.

Energiya is the largest, most powerful rocket ever built. The 198-foot (60-m)-tall rocket has four liquid-hydrogen/liquid oxygen-fueled engines that are supplemented by four strap-on liquid-fuel boosters, providing a total of 6.6 million pounds (3 million kg) of thrust. The boosters are equipped with parachutes so that they can be recovered and reused. Energiya is an independent rocket, so it can be used by itself to launch unmanned cargo containers into orbit.

Buran made its first test flight on November 10, 1986, with pilots Igor Volk and Riminitas Stankyavechus at the controls. During the 10-minute flight, the aerodynamic characteristics of the orbiter were tested. Since this was a suborbital flight, *Buran* was equipped with jet engines.

105

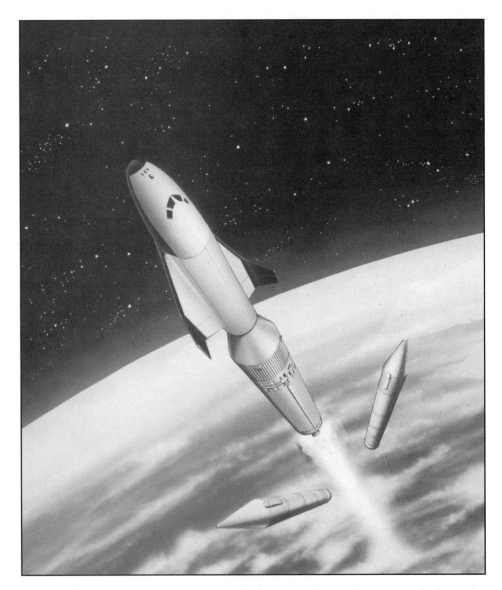

This illustration of the Hermes *space shuttle shows the spacecraft that scientists at the European Space Agency planned to build.*

On November 15, 1989—after 10 years of development and an investment of $10 billion—*Buran* was launched on its first unmanned orbital test flight. Although *Buran* made a perfect automatic landing, neither the Soviet shuttle nor Energiya ever flew again. The Soviet Union simply ran out of money. It wasn't long before the mighty nation fell apart.

Other Countries Think About Space Shuttles

Japan, France, Great Britain, and Germany have all proposed space shuttles and space planes of their own. France had plans to build a shuttle called *Hermes* that would have been similar to the American *Dyna-Soar*. The vehicle, which would have been launched on an upgraded Ariane 5 booster, would have had a three-person crew and been able to carry a 3-ton payload.

The British proposed the *HOTOL* (Horizontal Take-off and Landing), an unpiloted aircraft that would have taken off from—and landed on—a runway just like a conventional airplane. *HOTOL*'s cargo bay was about the same size as that of the Space Shuttle. If *HOTOL* needed to carry passengers, they could ride in a special compartment that fit into the cargo bay.

The Germans had plans for a fabulous-looking spaceplane called the *Sänger II*—a two-stage vehicle with entirely reusable parts. The first stage was a 165-foot (50-m)-long delta-winged aircraft that carried a smaller orbiter—the second stage—on its back. The Sänger II took off from a runway, and by the time it reached an altitude of 20 miles (32 km), it would be moving at 7,500 mph (12,070 km/hr). At this point, it launched the piggyback orbiter. The first stage would then return to Earth and land like a conventional airplane. The second stage, which also had wings, would continue on into orbit. When its mission was completed, it would also return to Earth and land like a conventional aircraft.

Unfortunately, none of these spaceships were ever built. The United States has also canceled some of its plans for new spacecraft. For example, at one point the United States was considering plans for the X-30 National Aero-Space Plane (NASP)—sometimes called the *Orient Express* because it could travel from the United States to Japan in just a few minutes. This long, narrow, wedge-shaped vehicle would have taken off from a runway using conventional jet engines and then switched over to scramjet engines. A single rocket engine would eventually give it the additional boost it needed to achieve orbit.

9

ROCKETS TODAY AND TOMORROW

Scientists and engineers at NASA and at private companies continue to look for ways to design inexpensive, reusable spacecraft. Researchers at McDonnell Douglas, a private aerospace firm, are working on a rocket that would take off vertically, fly directly into orbit, deliver its cargo, and land tail-first at its launch site. A 40-foot (12-m) model of this spacecraft, called the DC-X, was built and tested at White Sands, New Mexico, with great success.

It is very strange to watch one of these tests. The rocket rises slowly, comes to a complete stop in mid-air, and hovers on the blast from its four engines for a short time. Next, it tips to one side and moves parallel to the ground for a few hundred feet before stopping again. Then, the DC-X does something no other rocket in history has ever done—it lowers itself to the ground, coming to a gentle tail-first landing on its four stubby legs.

The most remarkable thing about the DC-X is not immediately apparent, however. The rocket was built almost entirely from off-the-shelf parts. Its engines are those used in the Centaur rocket; its navigational equipment comes from the F-15 Eagle fighter jet; and its hinges and hatch-closing springs are from Kmart and Home Depot! Not having to design and invent every part from scratch meant that the DC-X could be built very cheaply and reliably.

McDonnell Douglas hoped that the DC-X tests would lead to a government contract to build a full-size version—the LV-109 *Millennium Express*—an 80-foot (24-m)-tall, cone-shaped rocket. Atop this would have been a cylindrical second stage that could carry a six-person orbital crew ferry, a two-person Apollo-type crew capsule, or a cargo container. Unfortunately, the DC-X had difficulty finding government funding and, after a disastrous fire destroyed a flight model, the program was canceled in late 1996.

The DC-X's leading contender as the new post-shuttle NASA space vehicle was the Lockheed Martin X-33 spacecraft, which won the coveted government contract in July 1996. The X-33 is a wedge-shaped, "lifting body" spacecraft. In other words, its entire body acts like a wing, supporting the spacecraft as it glides back into Earth's atmosphere. The X-33 takes off vertically and lands horizontally, like a conventional aircraft. If the X-33 test vehicle proves successful, it will be developed into the full-size *VentureStar* orbiter.

McDonnell Douglas and Lockheed Martin are not the only private companies interested in developing spacecraft. The Pegasus launch vehicle was designed and built by the Orbital Sciences Corporation. This three-stage rocket is carried beneath the wing of a B-52 bomber to an altitude of 40,000 feet (12,192 m). It can then propel itself and a small satellite into orbit.

Robert Zubrin's planned *Rocketplane* is a small spaceplane about the size of a fighter jet. Carrying a full load of kerosene fuel, it would take off from a runway. When it reaches an altitude of about 30,000 feet (9,144 m), it would meet with a

An artist's representation of the Lockheed Martin X-33

tanker and take on a load of liquid oxygen to replace the spent kerosene. The *Rocketplane* would then switch over to its rocket engine—burning kerosene and liquid oxygen—and continue into space. Although the spaceplane will be used primarily to put satellites into orbit, a slightly enlarged version could carry passengers from Los Angeles to London in just 40 minutes. The ride would cost about twice as much as an ordinary plane ticket.

An even more unusual concept is that of the *Roton,* invented by Bevin McKinney and Gary Hudson. It is a combination of a helicopter and a rocket that looks something like a stubby V-2 with four helicopter blades near its nose. Small rockets near the tips of the blades make them rotate (like water rotates in a spinning lawn sprinkler). Since this "helicopter" does not need atmospheric oxygen to fly, it can attain a very high altitude. When it reaches a height at which there is too little air for the blades to function, the *Roton* switches over to its rocket engine and continues on into orbit. To return to Earth, the spacecraft more or less reverses the procedure. When it drops into an area of the atmosphere that is dense enough for the blades to operate, they start spinning. This helps to slow the spacecraft's fall. Eventually, using a combination of its rocket-powered rotors and its main engine, *Roton* lands tail-first. *Roton* can take off and land almost anywhere—even a small local airport could handle it. It doesn't need any special ground support or launchpad.

Many aerospace companies in the United States and other countries are interested in the possibility of space tourism. Several Japanese companies have joined forces to design and build a rocket large enough to carry several dozen passengers into space. Other companies are working on rockets that would carry fewer passengers. In most cases, tourist flights would not be orbital, but passengers would be able to see Earth in the midst of a black sky and experience weightlessness.

The Future of the Rocket

According to Newton's Third Law of Motion, anything that ejects material in one direction will move in the opposite direction. Scientists are using this knowledge to create a new generation of rockets that are very different from those in use today.

These rockets will be powered by electrons, ions, electromagnets, or nuclear power.

Most likely, rocket development will take two different directions. Some researchers will develop rockets to power spacecraft that will explore and colonize the Moon and the planets in our solar system. Other scientists and engineers will concentrate on rockets used for space tourism. Even now, several private companies are taking space tourism very seriously. It many not be too long before you can buy a ticket to orbit Earth.

In the meantime, rockets will continue to perform many important jobs. Sounding rockets will provide information about the weather, upper atmosphere, and pollution. Launch vehicles will continue to place communications and navigational satellites in orbit, propel spacecraft to other worlds, and carry probes to the far reaches of the solar system. And, of course, all these rockets will thrill and inspire us—as they have for hundreds of years.

APPENDIX

Significant Rockets and Launch Dates		
Rocket Type	Nation that Developed	Year of First Launch
V-2	Germany	1942
Jupiter C	United States	1956
A series	Soviet Union	1957
Vanguard	United States	1958
Thor-Able	United States	1958
Atlas	United States	1959
Mercury-Redstone	United States	1961
Scout	United States	1962
Delta series	United States	1962
D series	Soviet Union	1965
Diamant series	France	1965
Titan 3	United States	1966
Lambda 4S	Japan	1966
Saturn series	United States	1967
Black Arrow	Great Britain	1969
Mu series	Japan	1970
N series	Japan	1975
Ariane series	European Space Agency	1979
SLV-3	India	1980
Space Shuttle	United States	1981
Energiya	Soviet Union	1987
Buran	Soviet Union	1987
Long March series	China	1988
Shavit	Israel	1988

GLOSSARY

acceleration—any change in velocity or direction.

antipodal—points on the globe that are exactly opposite one another. The spaceplane designed by Eugen Sänger was called an antipodal bomber because it would have been capable of bombing a target on the opposite side of Earth from where it took off.

astronautics—the science and technology of spaceflight.

ballistic missile—missile whose trajectory (path) is determined entirely by the pull of gravity and the friction of the air. A stone thrown into the air follows a ballistic trajectory, as does the bullet fired from a gun.

bazooka—a weapon that allows a soldier to safely fire a rocket at a distant target. Basically, it is a hollow tube, open at both ends. The soldier holds it on his or her shoulder and points it toward the target. Another soldier inserts the rocket in the rear end of the tube and the first soldier fires it by pulling a trigger.

booster—a rocket used to give another rocket—or even an airplane—the acceleration it needs for takeoff. This is similar to the idea behind a launch vehicle, except that a booster rocket is usually an extra attachment, rather than a rocket in its own right. The solid-fuel rockets attached to the sides of the Space Shuttle are boosters that help it take off.

center of gravity—the point at which an object balances perfectly.

centrifugal force—the force that seems to push objects away from the center of their rotation. When you are on a spinning carousel, the force that seems to push you away from the middle is centrifugal force.

escape velocity—the speed at which an object must travel to escape from a celestial body's gravity forever. Escape velocity depends on the body a rocket is lifting off from. Earth's escape velocity is 7 miles/second (11.2 km/sec.). Planets with more or less gravity than Earth have different escape velocities.

fuel—any material that can be combined with an oxidizer to yield the hot gases that propel a rocket. A fuel can be solid or liquid. Almost anything that can burn has been used as rocket fuel at one time or another, from gasoline, kerosene, and fuel oil to liquid hydrogen and powdered aluminum.

hybrid rocket—a rocket that uses a special combination of propellants that are physically dissimilar. For example, some hybrid rockets use a solid fuel and a liquid oxidizer.

launch vehicle—a rocket whose purpose is to launch another rocket or spacecraft away from Earth. Many military rockets have been converted into very successful launch vehicles.

liquid-fuel rocket—a rocket that keeps its fuel and oxidizer in liquid form. This kind of rocket is very powerful and can be stopped and restarted. As a result, it is much more complicated and expensive than a solid-fuel rocket. The Space Shuttle's main engines are liquid-fuel rocket motors. They burn liquid oxygen and liquid hydrogen.

multistage rocket—a rocket made up of reusable smaller sections. When the fuel in one stage is used up, it detaches. The engine in the next stage continues to propel the rocket.

Mach—a unit used to measure speed relative to the speed of sound. Mach 1 is the speed of sound, Mach 2 is twice the speed of sound, Mach 0.5 is half the speed of sound.

orbit—(noun) the path that one object follows when going around another. A perfectly circular orbit is rare—most are elliptical.

orbit—(verb) to move around an object. The Moon orbits Earth, and Earth orbits the sun.

oxidizer—any substance containing oxygen that will allow fuel to burn.

payload—how much a rocket can carry.

propellant—any substance, or combination of substances, that supplies the mass that a rocket motor ejects to propel forward. In most rockets, the propellant is the fuel and oxidizer.

pyrotechnics—the art and science of fireworks.

recoil—to move back as described by Newton's Third Law of Motion.

rifle—the technique of putting curved grooves inside the barrel of a gun.

rotary rocket—a rocket that spins rapidly as it flies. It flies straighter and with more accuracy than other rockets.

solid-fuel rocket—a rocket with fuel that is a powder or solid material and contains its own supply of oxygen. Solid-fuel rockets are much simpler and cheaper to make than liquid-fuel rockets, but they cannot be turned off or controlled once they've been started. The Space Shuttle's giant strap-on boosters are solid-fuel rockets.

sounding rocket—rockets used for atmospheric research.

space shuttle—any spacecraft designed to carry people and cargo into and back from orbit. A space shuttle can be a multi-stage spacecraft like the U.S. Space Shuttle or it can be a single-stage rocket or spaceplane.

spaceplane—a spacecraft designed to take off and land like an ordinary airplane.

suborbital—a rocket that does not achieve a fast enough speed to escape from Earth's gravity. It falls back to Earth rather than beginning to orbit around Earth.

thrust—how hard an engine can push.

vacuum—a space or volume that contains nothing at all.

vane—a small metal or ceramic blade that can be put in the exhaust nozzle of a rocket. If a vane is set at an angle, exhaust will come out of the nozzle at an angle and the rocket will spin.

RESOURCES

BOOKS

Baker, David. *Spaceflight and Rocketry*: A Chronology. New York: Facts on File, 1996.

Chartrand, Mark. *Exploring Space*. New York: Golden Press, 1991.

Lehman, Milton. *Robert H. Goddard*. New York: Da Capo, 1988.

Miller, Ron. *The Dream Machines*. Malabar, FL: Kreiger Publishing Co., 1993.

Ordway, Frederick I., III and Mitchell Sharpe. *The Rocket Team*. New York: Crowell, 1979.

Stuhlinger, Ernst and Frederick I. Ordway III. *Wernher von Braun: Crusader for Space*. Malabar, FL: Krieger Publishing Co., 1994.

von Braun, Wernher, Frederick I. Ordway III, and Dave Dooling. *Space Travel—A History*. New York: Harper & Row, 1985.

Winter, Frank H. *Rockets Into Space*. Cambridge, MA: Harvard University Press, 1990.

_____. *The First Golden Age of Rocketry*. Washington, D.C.: Smithsonian Institution Press, 1990.

_____. *Prelude to the Space Age*. Washington, D.C.: Smithsonian Institution Press, 1983.

WEB SITES

There is a vast number of sites on the Internet devoted to space and rocketry. A good way to find most of these sites is to consult Yahoo's space index at **www.yahoo.com/science/space/**. A selection of interesting or useful sites is listed below.

Model rocketry is a safe, popular hobby. The National Association of Rocketry has many local chapters that hold meetings regularly. To find out more about the organization and the contests it sponsors or to read their recommended rules of safety, visit their web site.
www.nar.org

A guide to the present locations of historic rockets and spacecraft.
www.yourlink.net/gerard/fieldguide/index.html

The official NASA history site with information on every NASA space mission as well as overall information on the general history of space travel.
www.ksc.nasa.gov/history/history.html

The official NASA Space Shuttle web site. It includes the history of the shuttle program and upcoming missions.
http://shuttle.nasa.gov/

Official information about the X-33 spacecraft program.
http://rlv.msfc.nasa.gov/x33/index.html

Web page of Kelly Space & Technology, a private company that is trying to develop an inexpensive launch vehicle.
www.kellyspace.com

Information about the spacecraft that Kistler Aerospace Corp. wants to build.
www.newspace.com/industry/kistler/std/specs.htm

Web page for the Pioneer Pathfinder spaceplane.
www.rocketplane.com/

Web page for the *Roton* rotary launch vehicle.
www.rotaryrocket.com/

The history of space exploration.
http://bang.lanl.gov/solarsys/history.htm

This week in space history . . .
www.sji.org/ed/spchist/html

Web page devoted to the X Prize, which will award $10 million to the builder of the first privately built rocket to twice carry human passengers to an altitude of 62 miles (100 km).
www.xprize.com

INDEX

ABOUT THE AUTHOR

Ron Miller is an author and illustrator who concentrates on topics related to space and space travel. He is a contributing editor for *Air & Space/Smithsonian* magazine, a member of the International Academy of Astronautics, a Life Member and a past Trustee of the International Association for the Astronomical Arts, a member of the North American Jules Verne Society, and a Fellow of the British Interplanetary Society.

Miller has written many magazine articles and close to twenty books, including *The Grand Tour, Cycles of Fire, In the Stream of Stars*, and the *History of Earth, The Dream Machines*, and a trilogy of fantasy novels. His illustrations have appeared on dozens of book jackets and in such magazines as *National Geographic, Reader's Digest, Smithsonian, Air & Space*, and *Sky & Telescope*. Miller has worked as a production illustrator for several motion pictures, including *Dune* and *Total Recall*. He has also designed a set of ten commemorative stamps for the U.S. Postal Service. Miller lives in Fredericksburg, Virginia.